Coping with Stress for Mental and Physical Health and Longevity

Bruce S. Rabin, M.D., Ph.D.

authorHOUSE®

AuthorHouse™
1663 Liberty Drive
Bloomington, IN 47403
www.authorhouse.com
Phone: 1 (800) 839-8640

Published by AuthorHouse 01/04/2019

ISBN: 978-1-5462-7407-0 (sc)
ISBN: 978-1-5462-7408-7 (hc)
ISBN: 978-1-5462-7413-1 (e)

Library of Congress Control Number: 2018915335

Print information available on the last page.

Contents

TO BEGIN, THERE ARE SOME THINGS I'D LIKE YOU TO KNOW

Please do not consider this journey that I will be taking you on as a book with a beginning and end. This is a journey that is continuous. There is no final destination because you always will want to use the behaviors and techniques that help you cope with stress and enhance the likelihood of your being mentally and physically healthy as you age.

What you will be reading and learning is a journey that will teach you how to change the way your brain responds to stress. The journey will:

1. provide education so that you understand why stress can alter both mental and physical health, and,
2. will teach you how to reduce the effect of stress on your mental and physical health.

There will always be things that cause you stress. No one can cause the stress you will experience to go away. Therefore, to improve the quality of your mental and physical health you need to change the way your brain responds to stress. My goal is to help you accomplish this.

I hope to present this journey as a conversation, so that you feel I'm talking to you. I have learned that this is the most effective way for me to communicate what I will be presenting to you.

I have 3 primary goals and I want you to be aware of these now. I also want you to know that sometimes you may be uncomfortable with what you are hearing. However, it is important to understand events that occur early in life define aspects of mental and physical health throughout life. Each of the 3 goals will be described in detail as you proceed:

1. Every person has the right to become all they are capable of becoming. Some of the factors that affect who we become include the stress a woman experiences during pregnancy, the amount of abuse a child experiences, and whether an individual is bullied.

2. Learning to increase your ability to manage stress will help you to stay healthy as you go thru the aging process. Stay healthy, get older, die quickly-that is the blessing. Yes, the longer you stay healthy as you age, the shorter your demise. I hope saying this doesn't make you uncomfortable. We all are going to die. Let's do all we can to avoid serious chronic disease, manage chronic disease better when it occurs, and increase the likelihood of staying healthy as we age. I consider that a blessing.

3. Developing the skills that increase your ability to cope with stress will help to make you a meaningful role model for others who will see how stress does not have to alter their mental and physical health. This is an especially important message if you have children and grandchildren.

You will soon be aware that I repeat myself. This is done on purpose. The way you will remember what I am trying to teach you is for you to hear it more than once. Once you have completed this journey let me hear whether my system of teaching works.

YOU PROBABLY (SHOULD) WANT TO KNOW WHO I AM AND WHY AM I WRITING THIS

BECAUSE, UNLESS YOU KNOW MY QUALIFICATIONS THERE IS NO RESON YOU SHOULD TRUST WHAT I WILL BE TELLING YOU

FIRST A FORMAL INTRODUCTION:

I am an Emeritus Professor at the University of Pittsburgh. I joined the University of Pittsburgh in 1972, and left in 2017, after 45 years, to spend more time helping people learn how to reduce the effect of stress on their health. I was Professor of Pathology and Psychiatry at the University of Pittsburgh and Medical Director of the Division of Clinical Immunopathology and the Healthy Lifestyle Program at the University of Pittsburgh Medical Center.

I have dedicated my professional life to understanding the immune system and the factors which influence it. I discovered early on that stress – a variable in every person's life – exerts a profound influence on the human immune system and health. From that point forward my work focused on the effects of stress on health and the pathways of communication between the brain and the immune system – the mind/body connection.

Equally important to my research, I have been instrumental in moving science and research to real-world applications by developing programs designed to help people identify, learn and adhere to behaviors that will maintain their wellness and lower their risk of developing serious and potentially life-threatening conditions and diseases.

With a career that has spanned 45 years, my work is widely referenced – from the scientific community to national news to local health care articles; I have been sought out to serve on a number of government panels to advance awareness and promote research in mind-body medicine. My research has yielded more than 300 publications, and my research laboratory has trained over 50 young scientists who are making their own contributions to medicine– which I consider my single-most significant accomplishment.

As a result of my work, people of all ages, socioeconomic levels, educational backgrounds and lifestyle - are learning more about how to more effectively cope with the stress in their lives; new approaches to disease have been understood; mind-body connections are more widely and universally recognized; and innovative approaches to health care management have emerged.

OK, NOW A MORE PERSONAL INTRODUCTION:

I have spent approximately 5 years planning this book. I started writing it many times, but I discarded most of what I wrote because it did not clearly convey the meaningful messages that I know are important. My writing was uneven. Sometimes sounding as if I was speaking to medical students and sometimes as if I was speaking to people who needed help coping with the stress in their lives.

I didn't feel that what I wrote would motivate all who read this to increase their ability to cope with stress (I will explain and clarify this as we go on) for your own health benefits and so that you would become a healthy lifestyle role model for others.

Eventually I understood my problem which was that I'm a better talker than a writer. When I speak to groups about how individuals can increase their ability to cope with stress they understand what I am telling them and why it is important. I have even been called a "show stopper" by a Federal Judge. However, when I wrote about how you can increase your ability to cope with stress it didn't sound meaningful and motivating to me. I found my writing to be a bit boring, sometimes quite boring. Eventually I realized that I must write this book as if I am talking to you. I hope I am going to be able to do that, because, if I can I believe I can have a positive effect on the quality of your mental and physical health as you go thru the aging process.

Another issue is that you need to be convinced that you should listen to me. What makes what I am going to tell you more meaningful than what you can find presented in other books that focus on stress coping? Why is this book different, why am I different than other writers?

- The first reason is that this is what I know a lot about. Not by reading about it, but by a leading a large research program that has contributed to our understanding of how stress affects health.
    - o I have been a meaningful contributor to the science of psychoneuroimmunology being one of the founders of the Psychoneuroimmunology Research Society (PNIRS) and a President of the PNIRS.
    - o I am also an immunologist having a PhD in immunology along with my MD. I was also a President of the Association of Medical Laboratory Immunologists. Thus, I know a lot about immunology and stress and health. I don't just

read about what others did and try to explain it. I can clearly explain the health significance of the mind-body connection, because I did the work!

- The second reason is that I have been fortunate, along with my colleague Irene Kane, PhD, to have developed and implemented many successful programs that help people reduce the effect of stress on their health. These programs have been provided to several thousand people in western Pennsylvania. Comments from participants in our programs are provided as you proceed.

  o We have taken what we learned in the laboratory and successfully moved it to the real world where I now help people increase the likelihood of remaining healthy as they go thru the aging process and, importantly, to become meaningful role models for those who are important to them.

  o We have also learned from those who have participated in our stress coping programs. The suggestions they have made have helped to refine the material being presented to you. As someone who was in the academic world for 45 years, it sometimes is difficult to explain health concepts in terms understandable to those not in the academic world. I have been fortunate to have had thousands of people in the programs I conducted helping me make sure I communicate well, so that what I have to say is easy to understand and is meaningful. In addition, I have the desire and passion to share what was learned with you.

It is this knowledge and experience that I want to talk to you and teach you about as we proceed.

Over the past decade many people have learned about stress and stress coping from me. Many readily and consistently use what I taught them, and many others do not. The usual reason for not engaging in the use of the stress coping techniques is that "I can handle it myself" and "I'm too old to change my life style". Both excuses are wrong.

With education and understanding of what stress is and how it affects health you will appreciate that we all can use help to reduce how stress affects our health and it is never too late to engage in behaviors that increase the quality of our health and life.

I hope you will become someone who I am able to motivate to consistently use what you will learn. That you will incorporate some of the behaviors and techniques I will teach you into your lifestyle. Please remember, it is not just for your benefit but if you become a healthy lifestyle role model for the children and/or grandchildren who love you, you have helped them and added meaning to your life.

To motivate you, the following are a few comments from participants in the stress coping programs that I share with you to let you know that I have done a lot more than research in stress and health. I've helped people (more comments are provided later):

- The class has taught me to use stress management techniques proactively instead of reactively. I still have stress in my life and in the workplace, but I am in control of my response to it.
- I found Dr. Rabin's course to be the broadest, all-encompassing, thorough, and potentially helpful course that I have ever taken. Notice that I say 'potentially helpful.' That is because I fully realize that managing my stress must come from me.
- Dr. Rabin had provided me with a detailed up-to-date road map. And I am grateful that he has done such a thorough and useful job of preparing it.
- Dr. Rabin helped me to finally understood the science of stress and how stress-management techniques turn off the flow of hormones. I began realizing how childhood problems made me psychologically predisposed to chronic stress.
- Stress has causes and understanding them is useful. You can treat this condition with his program. But another dimension to understanding it is that there's nothing wrong with me. I'm just a product of my environment and my life to this point. It's not a shortcoming.

- In my opinion, *everyone* should have the opportunity to experience this training.
- The classes have taught me invaluable skills that will continue to enrich and enhance not only the quality of my existence, but also that of my family. I wish this opportunity had come to me earlier in life.
- Sometimes our jobs do create stress within our lives. Being able to recognize these stresses and manage them help us to be more productive in our jobs and our home life.
- Your class has helped me to cope with stresses of everyday life, and I will continue to use the strategies for wellness that you have shown me. I am richer for having had this experience.
- In addition to the "advertised" benefits, I have had other positive side effects. I have had no cold sores (which I used to have almost constantly).
- I have greatly improved my relationships with my family and friends, and almost nothing which goes wrong seems to be a big deal to me anymore.
- I have noticed less of a need to eat sweet and salty snacks and an increased desire to walk and move around. At first I was hesitant about the "Wellness" Program that was offered to us, I knew I was stressed out, but I never though anything could be done about it. Now I know it was truly a blessing and that the participants are truly thankful that this program has been offered to us, a wonderful "Gift".
- At home, these techniques have helped me relate better with my children.

Be aware that many things you experience that cause you stress will always be there, they are not going away. **To reduce the effect of stress on your health you must change the way your brain responds to stress. We call this an increased ability to cope with stress. By being better able to cope with stress you will reduce the effect of stress on your mental and physical health.**

I want to repeat this, "To reduce the effect of stress on your health you must change the way your brain responds to stress". The journey I will take you on will accomplish this.

Use what you will learn to keep your stress hormone concentrations low (you will learn how to do this) and be rewarded by increasing the likelihood of a better quality of mental and physical health as you continue to age.

I ask you to:

- Use what you learn in this journey as often as possible so that it becomes a routine part of your life. The more often you use the behaviors and techniques you will be taught, the more effective they will become. Practice using them when you are calm and feeing good. If you do this, it becomes easier to use them when you experience stress.
- Share the information with those who are important to you. This will make it more likely that you will remind each other to use the stress coping techniques when you need to use them. Help each other.
- Tell others how the quality of your life is better when you increase your ability to cope with stress. I am confident that this will happen. They will listen to you and look upon you as a meaningful role model.
- Believe that you will succeed

IMPORTANT THINGS I WANT
YOU TO BE AWARE OF

- When children are born they do not know which behaviors promote good health and which do not.
- Children learn their behaviors from the people that are important to them. They learn from their role models. Therefore, it is important for parents, grandparents, teachers, and all who interact with children, to be healthy lifestyle role models and demonstrate

to children that they do more than talk about healthy haviors, they actually do them.

- The behaviors we learn and use when we are young I call our default behaviors, i.e., the behaviors we tend to use throughout life. These default behaviors influence the quality of our long term mental and physical health.

- If we used healthy lifestyle behaviors from the earliest stages of life, these would likely be the default behaviors we use throughout life. Then when we are older we would not have to be concerned about changing from unhealthy to healthy lifestyle behaviors. You know how hard it is to change behavior. We all try and rarely succeed. Think about increasing the amount of physical activity you do. If we were physically active from the earliest times of life we would likely be physically active throughout life.

- For the reasons I have just stated it is critical that children use healthy lifestyle behaviors from the youngest ages and do this because their role models, including parents, other family members, clergy, and teachers are using them.

THE HEALTHY LIFESTYLE BEHAVIORS INCLUDE:

o   Coping with stress
o   Not smoking
o   Being physically active
o   Not being overweight
o   Eating a health enhancing diet including fruits, vegetables, and grains to the best of your ability (I use the phrase 'to the best of your ability' because I know that doing this can cost more than one has the financial resources for. This, in my opinion, is not fair).

WHO WILL BENEFIT FROM THIS
STRESS COPING JOURNEY?

- Healthy individuals who want to increase their likelihood of staying healthy as they age. Remember, the longer you stay healthy as you age the happier you will be as it will be less likely that you will have to cope with health problems.

- Pregnant women who want to decrease the concentration of stress hormones in their blood (I will talk more about this later).
- Those with young children to help them cope with the stress of raising children so that they are calm, not impulsive, and do not expose the children to anger and inconsistent behaviors.
- Parents, grandparents, and teachers who if they learn to help children cope with stress will likely have a positive effect on their own health.
- Anyone who works in a high stress environment. This includes first responders, police officers, and firefighters. Using stress coping behaviors will, when in a workplace or work situation with elevated levels of stress, reduce your risk of stress related health problems, including the risk of having a heart attack.
- Those with diabetes who will achieve better control of their glucose levels.
- Individuals who have experienced high levels of stress in the past, such as Veterans of combat.
- Those with disease caused by the immune system. An increased ability to cope with stress will reduce the clinical severity of the disease and reduce the frequency of having a relapse. These diseases include:
  o Rheumatoid arthritis
  o Multiple sclerosis
  o Psoriasis
  o Ulcerative colitis
  o Crohn's disease
- Individuals with:
  o Depression
  o Chronic fatigue syndrome
  o Irritable bowel syndrome
  o Fibromyalgia
  o Cancer

Actually, anyone who has stress in their life can achieve a better quality of mental and physical health by increasing their ability to cope with stress.

My hope for you is that because of your taking this journey:

- the likelihood of your remaining healthy as you continue to age will increase
- your likelihood of becoming a meaningful healthy lifestyle role model for others will increase.

Yes, your behavior can influence how others behave. Those close to you may want to be more like you. An example, and I recognize that this is extreme, is that when someone wins the lottery their neighbors start to spend more money, even if they don't have it to spend. Another example is that if you have a friend who becomes obese, the likelihood of your gaining weight increases. Thus, engage in healthy lifestyle behaviors and let your friends know how good they make you feel. Hopefully, they will want to be like you.

PLEASE READ THIS MESSAGE ABOUT BEING OVERWHELMED

People who have participated in our programs tell me that there can be a lot of stress caused when they try to reduce their response to stress. They tell me that they try a stress coping technique for a short time and don't feel that it helps them. They then try something else. Then they start to worry that they won't be successful. They are shopping for something that works quickly and if they don't find something, they start browsing. My message is, be patient.

The use of behaviors and techniques that increase your ability to cope with stress take time and repetition to become successful. Everything I am going to tell you works. Remember, the goal of whatever you do is to reduce the concentration of stress hormones in your blood. To do this you have to change the way your brain responds to stress. It doesn't happen in a day. It takes time and practice. However, when you are successful you will enhance the quality of your mental and physical health.

Everything that I will be providing to you is easy to do. If not, you wouldn't do it. Here is a comment from someone who participated in our stress coping program: "I have greatly improved my relationships with my family and friends, and almost nothing which goes wrong seems to be a big deal to me anymore". Additional comments are provided at the end of this journey. I am providing these for you to convince you that you are not wasting your time taking this journey.

Be patient. Know that what you are learning works.

MORE MOTIVATION TO HELP YOU WANT TO INCREASE YOUR ABILITY TO COPE WITH STRESS

It's hard to imagine that most people are not aware that:

- smoking cigarettes increases the risk of developing lung cancer
- being overweight and not physically active increases the risk of developing type 2 diabetes
- driving while drunk puts people, in addition to the drunk driver, at risk of being harmed

Yet, people still smoke, children are overweight and sedentary, and people drive drunk.

My point is that knowledge alone may not be enough to convince people to engage in healthy lifestyle behaviors. That is why it is critical for me to motivate you to want to use the behaviors and techniques that will reduce the response of your brain to stress and that will increase the likelihood of your having a high quality of mental and physical health as you age.

The most consistent thing that people who have participated in my stress coping programs tell me is that the following statement is what had the greatest impact on their wanting to use healthy lifestyle behaviors:

"The longer you stay health as you continue to age leaves less time to develop a chronic disease before you die. Therefore, the goal is to stay health, grow older, and then have a short demise. That is the blessing you want to achieve." Stay healthy, grow older, die quickly. As I said before, I hope this isn't upsetting to you. We are all going to die and let's do all we can to be as healthy as possible until then.

OK. Let's be realistic. There are no guarantees that by engaging in healthy lifestyle practices you will stay healthy as you continue to age. However, the odds change in your favor. There is less risk of depression, more times of feeling good and finding more joy in life is wonderful. Thinking clearly, focusing, being efficient in what you do, being a healthy lifestyle role model for those who are important to you, are all likely to occur.

If you have children and/or grandchildren think about how they see you react when you experience stress. Do you want them to see you losing your cool, yelling, saying things that are inappropriate? Or do you want them to see you acknowledge that something is causing you stress and you're then telling them that, for example, you are going to take 3 deep breathes and then you will figure out what to do to handle the situation. Thus, there is more to be achieved than just staying healthy as you continue to age. You will be a role model for others.

Many who will take this journey may already have a chronic medical condition. If the medical condition is caused by an autoimmune disease it is likely that the course of the disease will be less severe, and the duration of remission will be longer. If the disease is a malignancy the course of disease may be affected in a positive way by improving the function of the immune system. Also, the perception of pain associated with a disease may be less when using stress coping techniques. Thus, there are benefits to those who are already affected by a disease.

Also remember that it is often difficult to change from using an unhealthy lifestyle behavior to a healthy behavior if we are doing it for our own benefit. But when you become a healthy lifestyle role model for those you love and care about, it becomes easier for you to sustain changes in behavior. Now you are not only changing behavior for your own benefit, you are also doing it for those who are important to you.

NOW I WILL DEFINE STRESS IN A WAY THAT WILL ALLOW YOU TO VISUALIZE HOW STRESS CAN ALTER THE QUALITY OF YOUR HEALTH

For our purpose the definition of stress is, "something that happens to you or something that you experience exceeds the capability of your brain to effectively cope with the event".

When you experience stress, the stress will:

1. Activate several areas of your brain we call the 'stress reactive' areas.
2. This will cause an elevation in the concentration of several hormones in your blood.
3. The principal stress hormones are cortisol, epinephrine, and norepinephrine.
4. It is the elevation of these hormones whose concentration is regulated by stress, that cause the mental and physical health alterations associated with stress.

Being able to cope with stress means having the ability to reduce the effect of stress on mental and physical health. You will learn to do this by using behaviors and techniques that reduce the response of your brain to being activated when you experience something your brain considers to be stress.

THE BOTTOM LINE ABOUT STRESS COPING:

This journey will teach you how to increase your ability to cope with stress so that when your brain perceives something as stress there will be less activation of the stress-reactive areas of your brain. If there is less activation of the stress-reactive areas of your brain the elevation of the concentration of stress hormones will be reduced. If the concentration of the hormones is reduced there will be less of a negative effect on your health.

THIS IS SO CRITICAL TO UNDERSTAND THAT I WILL SAY IT AGAIN

The effect of stress on mental and physical health is due to the elevation in the concentration of the stress hormones that occur when the stress reactive areas of the brain are activated

AN ILLUSTTRATION OF THE BRAIN AND STRESS PERCEPTION

In the following diagram, the brain is shown to be affected by stress. If your brain considers something that you experience as stress, areas of your brain that respond to stress (the stress reactive brain areas) will become active. The principle stress reactive brain areas are called the paraventricular nucleus of the hypothalamus and the locus coeruleus (no need to memorize these names, just know that you have them in your brain). When these brain areas are activated by stress there will be an elevation in the concentration of several hormones in your blood (the names are glucocorticoid (also known as cortisol) and catecholamine (also known as epinephrine and norepinephrine). **It is the elevation of these hormones that will have an effect on both your mental health and your physical health.**

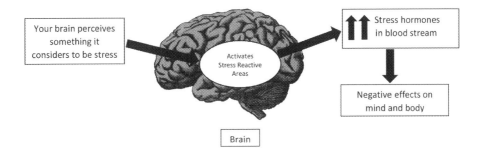

Coping with stress means that you use behaviors and techniques (that you will learn as you proceed thru this journey) to keep the stress reactive areas of your brain calm when your brain considers something to be stress.

That's all there is to it. Use the behaviors and techniques that reduce the response of your brain to stress and you will improve the quality of your mental and physical health and increase the likelihood of staying healthy as you age.

It is important to be aware that sometimes the stress may be so strong that none of your stress coping skills will work. For example, learning that a child has cancer. I'm sure you can think of many other examples. However, my goal is to teach you how to decrease the effect of events you encounter throughout the day on activating your stress reactive brain areas. Increasing our ability to cope with stress is how you will have a better quality of mental and physical health as you go thru the aging process. That is what you want.

I WANT YOU TO KNOW ABOUT SOME THINGS THAT CONTRIBUTE TO MAKING US WHO WE ARE

A very straight forward statement is, "When all children start kindergarten they should be at the same level in regard to learning ability and behavior". Very logical and hard to disagree with. However, be aware that abuse early in life (physical, mental, sexual or being neglected) experienced by children has been linked to alterations of the anatomy, physiology, and function of the brain of young children that may persist when they are adults.

The effects of abuse on the mind include an increased risk of having an altered learning ability, difficulty controlling behavior, and an increased risk of developing depression. Physical health effects include an increased risk of developing diabetes, heart disease, and immune system abnormalities. The more abuse (both in regard to severity and chronicity), the greater the risk of mental and physical health problems for the child.

To achieve the goal of all children having the same ability to learn and behave when they enter kindergarten will require eliminating abusive behavior toward children. When I am at a bus stop and I see a parent yelling at a child and telling them they are 'bad', sometimes grabbing and shaking them, I imagine that child 30 years later. It's not a pretty picture.

The following is a quote from Oprah Winfrey, someone who was abused as a child, but yet she shows that the deleterious effects do not have to occur. This is important to remember. Even if early life abuse occurs, the effects may not be permanent. Having caring and loving people who reach out to and support the victim of abuse can contribute to reducing the negative effects of abuse on both mental and physical health.

> Oprah said. "What I recognize is that a lot of people working in the philanthropic world, who are trying to help disadvantaged, challenged people from backgrounds that have been disenfranchised, are working on the wrong thing." While there have been plenty of job and training programs to help the disadvantaged, Winfrey said, "If you don't fix the hole in the soul, the thing that is where the wounds started, you're working at the wrong thing."

> "See, we go through life and we see kids who are misbehaving. 'Your juvenile delinquents,' we label them. And really the question that we should be asking is not 'what's wrong with that child' but 'what happened to that child?' The most important question you can ask of anybody instead of what's the matter with that kid, I say what happened to that child?"

Once again: "The most important question you can ask of anybody instead of what's the matter with that kid, I say what happened to that child?"

ANSWERS TO SOME QUESTIONS YOU MAY ASK: IF STRESS IS CAPABLE OF IMPAIRING YOUR HEALTH, WHY NOT JUST AVOID IT?

Sometimes we can avoid stress. If we know that someone is angry with us, we can avoid seeing them until they calm down. However, much of life's stress is unavoidable, such as divorce (maybe its unavoidable, maybe it isn't), losing one's job, an angry employer, children that get into trouble, caring for a relative with a serious disease, preparing for an exam at school. Even positive life enhancing experiences like moving to a new home or getting a new job can cause stress. When we change the conditions and circumstances of our lives, we must learn new skills which often produce stress. Thus, there is stress in our lives that is unavoidable.

IS THERE ONLY ONE WAY THAT I CAN LOWER THE CONCENTRATION OF THE STRESS HORMONES IN MY BLOOD? THE ANSWER IS NO:

There are several techniques that you will learn that decrease the concentration of stress hormones in your blood. I will teach these to you.

- Some have a rapid onset and are useful when you need a quick calming effect. An excellent example is taking deep breaths to increase the amount of oxygen in your blood.
- Others train your mind to become less responsive to stress and readjust your mind so that your baseline level of stress hormones is lower. Regular relaxation results in long-term changes that counteract the harmful effects of stress throughout the day. Examples are meditation and listening to guided imagery.

DO I NEED TO DO ALL THE THINGS THAT YOU WILL TEACH ME? THE ANSWER IS NO:

The journey you are participating in is designed to give you a chance to experience different techniques. For many people a combination of techniques becomes part of a personal health regimen. For others, one or two of the techniques will prove to be most helpful. You will experience the different techniques and then you will decide. My telling you what you must do will only create stress for you.

Not every technique may be suitable for you. Different individuals will be more comfortable and find it easier to do different techniques. THERE IS NO RIGHT OR WRONG WAY. WHAT IS IMPORTANT IS DOING IT!!!!

IS STRESS ALWAYS BAD? THE ANSWER IS NO:

Some aspects of the stress response have an important function. If you were stressed because of a dangerous situation, the changes in your body would help you flee to safety. When you experience stress, blood flow to muscle increases and the concentration of sugar in blood increases. This gives us the strength and energy to escape danger.

WHAT ELSE IS IMPORTANT TO KNOW ABOUT THE TECHNIQUES YOU WILL LEARN?

- You should practice them when you are calm and happy. It will be easier to use them when needed if you practice them when you are calm. It will also be easier to remember to use them when you need to use them.
- Have no fixed expectations or goals, otherwise the cure becomes the stressor! Eventually (it may take 3-6 months) you will find that the techniques just happen, without having to think about using them.

ALWAYS REMEMBER: Learning to cope with stress will not make you a less effective person or negatively affect your work performance. In fact, learning to cope with stress will make you more efficient in your everyday life, increase your feeling of calmness, and may even enhance your interaction with others.

Enough talking. Let's do something and get right to one of the most commonly used techniques that will rapidly lower the concentration of stress hormones. This will be repeated later when we focus on how to cope with acute stress.

DEEP BREATHING FOR CALMING YOURSELF WHEN EXPERIENCING AN ACUTE STRESSOR (THIS WE WILL BE REPEATED AGAIN LATER)

Deep breathing is a technique that you will be able to use to calm your mind, reduce the concentration of stress hormones in your blood, and contribute to an enhancement of your health. Deep breathing is a commonly used technique that many people use.

When we experience stress or something unexpected happens we often hold our breath or decrease how deeply we inhale. When we do this carbon dioxide increases in our blood and causes the brain to release a stress hormone (norepinephrine) that interferes with our ability to think clearly. In addition, the hormone causes blood pressure to rise. However, our main concern here is that it reduces our ability to think clearly and to focus. This may be the reason why we engage in impulsive behavior when we are experiencing stress. We may do something that later on we wish we hadn't done.

Deep breathing is exactly what it says. Take a deep breath to get more air into your lungs which will allow more oxygen to enter your blood. When you increase the amount of oxygen in your blood, your brain will detect the increased oxygen and will respond by decreasing the concentration of stress hormones in the blood.

USE THE FOLLOWING TO LEARN HOW TO INCREASE THE VOLUME OF AIR FLOWING INTO YOUR LUNGS

The essential point is that by pushing the wall of your abdomen out when you inhale, your diaphragm (the muscle that separates your chest from your abdomen) will drop, increasing the space that the lungs can expand into. This maximizes the flow of air into the lungs and of oxygen into the blood.

DEEP BREATHING INSTRUCTIONS:

1. Take a deeper inhalation breath than you usually do. To do this feel your abdominal wall pushing out as you breathe in. Make sure you are comfortable while doing this. How fast or slow you do it is up to you. Remember, what you are doing is increasing the volume of air entering your lungs. The only way to get more oxygen into your blood is to increase the amount of air entering your lungs.

2. Exhale by pulling your abdominal wall inward. This will push the air out. How fast or slow you do it is up to you. When you have completed your exhalation, you can now do another inhalation.

3. Breathe through your nose or mouth. Whichever is more comfortable. There are no rules, do what is comfortable for you.

4. Never take more than five deep breaths. If you feel a little dizzy, take fewer deep breaths. Usually you will feel calm and thinking clearly after taking 3 deep breaths.

5. If you still feel that you need to do more wait 15 minutes before doing it again. However, it is unlikely you will have to repeat it.

It is **important to emphasize** that you should PRACTICE this technique when you are calm and relaxed to increase your ability to do it when needed. It is hard to do a relaxation technique without practicing it. So please practice when you are calm. Then it is there for your use when you need it. Increasing your ability to cope with stress will make you more efficient in your everyday life and better equipped to deal with life's stresses and challenges.

- Please be aware that when your mind perceives something as stress it is difficult to think clearly. Thus, you may not remember to take 3-5 deep breaths.
- **Therefore, share this technique with your family and friends. When they see that you are upset they can remind you to deep**

breath and when you see that they are upset you can remind them.

Take your time, there is no hurry, spend as much time as you like on practicing deep breathing, the goal is to learn and increase your ability to cope with stress, don't cause stress for yourself, patience and repetition will benefit you

IT IS IMPORTANT TO REMEMBER THIS: We cannot make the stress in your life go away but we can change the way your brain responds to stress. By being better able to cope with stress you will have less of an elevation of stress hormones. It is the elevation of the stress hormones that alters your mental and physical health.

Testimonials about deep breathing from people who have participated in this stress coping program:

- As soon as I feel stressed, I think oh I need to belly breathe and I do and instantly it helps to calm me.
- I give credit to my class for saving my relationship at home. It is amazing how important it is to breathe and walk away from a situation when one gets really angry and hurt.
- I have already experienced relief physically and emotionally from changes in my breathing alone.
- I am able to breathe when I get upset and not respond so quickly without thinking
- This past week I had a hospital procedure, as I lay on the operating table I was feeling anxious. Automatically I began to breathe and visualize. The procedure was done before I knew it and I realized how effective and useful the techniques I learned were.
- The littlest things would stress me out and I would say things that I really didn't want to say out loud and I use to be very impatient. I have learned to be way more laid back and to walk away and take a couple deep breaths
- Benefits that I've experienced: much less aggressive driving; less bothered by rush hour traffic; able to be calmer in interactions

with others; better listener; able through deep breathing to reduce post-surgical back pain; and improved sleep.

- Just taking a few seconds to do something as easy as "breathing" can make such a difference in your day to ease the stressors. I also find myself enjoying the "moment" more often, taking the time to appreciate situations that are very important in my life.

- I have taken the knowledge I received and have taught it to my husband who was very reluctant at first, but now I see him taking a few seconds to breathe before he deals with difficult situations.

- Learning to breathe has helped me with stressful situations at home and at work.

- I find myself continually using the deep breathing technique to get me through excessively busy times

- I forget to just breathe at times, and I didn't realize the impact this had on my health. I am now focusing on my breathing, which I needed with a busy schedule and the demands of a 10-month-old baby.

HEALTH BENEFITS OF COPING WITH STRESS

For motivation, let's list the health benefits of coping with stress. More details will follow. When you keep your stress hormones low by coping with stress, each of the health factors listed below improves. Everything gets better:

- You have less difficulty thinking clearly and focusing
- You are less likely to act impulsively
- You will be less likely to become depressed and have the 'blues'
- Your ability to remember things will increase
- Your heart will beat less rapidly
- Blood pressure will be lower
- There is less accumulation of cholesterol into the blood vessels of your heart reducing the risk of having a heart attack
- Blood platelets will not stick to each other reducing the risk of having a heart attack

- The function of the immune system is improved
- The ability of the body to heal wounds increases
- Diabetes is easier to manage
- Weight is easier to manage
- Telomeres on the ends of your chromosomes become longer and are associated with better health
- The amount of inflammation in the body decreases

THE EFFECT OF STRESS HORMONES ON BOTH THE BRAIN AND THE BODY

Now I want to provide you with more detailed information regarding the effects of stress on health. Please remember that the primary reason that stress affects health is because of the elevation of hormones that occur when something you perceive as stress activates the stress reactive brain areas. Increasing your ability to cope with stress changes the response of your brain to stress. If your brain responds less there will be less hormones produced and stress will have less of an effect on your health.

I want you to know how stress alters both your mental and physical health to increase your motivation to not only reduce the effect of stress on your health but to increase the likelihood that you will help those you love and who love you increase their ability to cope with stress.

Don't forget, it is not stress itself that affects your health, it is the hormones that stress causes to increase in concentration that are the actual factors that affect health. If you increase your ability to cope with stress your brain will be less responsive to stress, the hormonal response to stress will not be as great, and there will be less of a negative effect on your health.

Please remember that these are **POSSIBLE** effects and do not happen to everyone who experiences stress. Some people experience more health changes than others, and some have little if any health changes. As you continue reading you will gain insight into aspects of life that influence the response of your brain to stress. Some things that influence your brains response to stress include the experience of high levels of stress early in life, how satisfied you are with your social network, how physically fit you are, and your sense of humor.

Therefore, do not assume that the following health alterations must happen to you. Keep a positive attitude, see the glass as half-full rather than half-empty, be physically active, enjoy your friends. As we proceed through this journey, know that the healthy lifestyle behaviors you use will have the capability of maintaining and enhancing the quality of your mental and physical health.

THE EFFECTS OF AN ELEVATION OF STRESS HORMONES ON THE MIND

1. **YOU WILL HAVE DIFFICULTY THINKING CLEARLY AND FOCUSING AND YOU MAY BE MORE LIKELY TO ACT IMPULSIVELY** - when your brain perceives something as stress there is a rapid rise in the concentration of a hormone called norepinephrine. This occurs within seconds. The elevation of this hormone interferes with your ability to focus and think clearly. When this occurs it becomes more likely that you will act on an impulse rather than thoughtfully.

   We have all experienced this. When someone or something is upsetting, or, for example, someone cuts you off while driving, have you ever said or done something (such as make a gesture) that is very unlike you. Well, it's not you; it's what the elevation of the hormone does to you. I will teach you 3 techniques that you can use to rapidly lower the concentration of this hormone and to help you focus and think clearly. One of these is deep breathing, which I have already provided to you and explained why it helps to keep you calm and focused. As you proceed you will learn how to use humor and chanting to accomplish the same effect of rapidly lowering the concentration of stress hormones. If you'd like, please go back and review deep breathing.

2. **YOU BECOME DEPRESSED AND HAVE THE 'BLUES'**-
the development of feeling depressed caused by an elevation of
stress hormones occurs for 2 reasons:

a. A sustained elevation of cortisol (one of the hormones
whose concentration increases when your brain
perceives something as stress) will damage and reduce
the number of brain cells in an area of the brain called
the hippocampus. When the number of brain cells in
the hippocampus is reduced the result is that you will
experience depression. Nothing you can do about it, that's
the way it is. Fortunately, the hippocampus can generate
new brain cells throughout life. When the concentration
of cortisol is lowered the brain cells come back with the
lessening of your feelings of depression. This may differ
from your belief that when you are born you have all the
brain cells you will ever have. That is wrong. Indeed, our
brain is capable of growing new brain cells.

b. When the immune system is activated there are chemicals,
called cytokines, that are released from cells of the immune
system. The primary purpose of these cytokines is to
regulate the function of the immune system. However,
in addition, the cytokines gain access to the brain. When
they get to the brain they are capable of inducing feelings
of depression, fatigue, and an increased perception of pain.

This explains why, when you have an upper respiratory
viral infection, you feel tired, down in the dumps, and
everything aches. This is called 'sickness behavior'. What
is occurring is that the infection activates your immune
system whose purpose is to fight off the infection. While
doing this the immune system releases chemicals called
'cytokines'. In addition to helping the immune system do
its job, the cytokines cause you to feel tired, have the blues,
and perceive pain more than usual.

However, in most people, when the cytokines get to the brain there is a mechanism that allows them to shut off their release from the immune system. The cytokines do this by causing an elevation in the concentration of cortisol in blood. Cortisol does many good things, one of which is reducing the amount of cytokines released by cells of the immune system.

However, if this system doesn't work properly, because the cytokines getting to the brain don't cause an elevation of cortisol, cytokines continue to be produced by the immune system. This is an abnormal response. When cytokine release is continuous the feelings of depression, fatigue, and an increased perception of pain may persist for a long time. This alteration of the normal response is something that may occur in someone who has experienced a lot of stress early in life, such as physical, mental, or sexual abuse, or neglect.

3. **YOUR ABILITY TO REMEMBER THINGS MAY DECREASE** at a younger age than would occur if you could cope with stress. A sustained elevation of cortisol can damage brain cells in areas of the brain involved with memory. These include areas of the brain called the hippocampus and the amygdala. Thus, this is a mechanism, other than Alzheimer's dementia or vascular problems that can cause you to have memory problems as you age. Just another reason why you want to increase your ability to cope with stress and keep the concentration of your stress hormones low.

THE EFFECTS OF AN ELEVATION OF STRESS HORMONES ON THE BODY

1. **YOUR HEART BEATS MORE RAPIDLY**- Stress is one of several mechanisms that result in a rapid heart rate. Heart rate is regulated by the two branches of the nervous system. The sympathetic nervous system (which increases heart rate) and

the parasympathetic nervous system (which slows the heart rate). When experiencing stress the sympathetic nervous system increases its activity to increase heart rate which overrides the effects of the parasympathetic nervous system that tries to slow heart rate. When your heart rate increases you may experience dizziness, shortness of breath, light headedness, or chest pain. You may even faint.

2. **YOUR BLOOD PRESSURE INCREASES**- Stress hormones cause blood vessels to constrict and decrease their diameter. Essentially the tubes that are the blood vessels become narrowed. When this occurs blood is squeezed into a reduced space and the only thing that can happen is that the pressure inside the blood vessels must go up. Using stress coping behaviors and techniques to reduce the concentration of stress hormones will help to reduce blood pressure by reducing the concentration of the hormone that causes blood vessels to become narrow. Keep your stress hormones low and have lower blood pressure.

3. **THERE IS AN ENHANCED ACCUMULATION OF CHOLESTEROL IN THE BLOOD VESSELS OF YOUR HEART** which causes narrowing of blood vessels in the heart and less flow of blood to the heart muscle. That means there is less oxygen delivered to the heart muscle and an increased risk of having a heart attack. The accumulation of cholesterol in the blood vessels of the heart is called atherosclerosis.

Cholesterol movement into the walls of the blood vessels of the heart involves: (a) white blood cells that contain cholesterol, (b) sticking onto the walls of the blood vessels of the heart, (c) moving into the blood vessels, and (d) depositing cholesterol in the blood vessel.

This process occurs more rapidly when someone is under stress because the stress hormones increase the concentration of molecules that are just like Velcro, on the lining of the blood vessel wall. The white blood cells that transport cholesterol into the blood vessel stick to these Velcro-like molecules making it easier for the white blood cells to move into the wall of the blood vessel and deposit cholesterol there.

Thus, the stress hormone induced increase in the concentration of these Velcro-like molecules on the blood vessels of the heart are responsible for increasing the amount of cholesterol transported into the blood vessels of the heart. Keep your stress hormones low and accumulate less cholesterol in your heart.

4. **YOUR CHANCE OF HAVING A HEART ATTACK IS INCREASED**- One mechanism causing a heart attack is that a blood vessel in the heart gets plugged up. When this happens blood cannot supply heart muscle with oxygen and the heart may stop pumping blood to the body. As you've read above, stress hormones increase how rapidly cholesterol accumulates in the walls of blood vessels of the heart and leads to narrowing of the blood vessels.

    Plugging up of the blood vessels involves 'platelets'. Platelets are small particles in blood whose purpose is to help form a clot when you have a cut and stop the bleeding. Normally, these small platelets are floating in the blood, not attached to each other. However, they stick to each other and form clumps when the concentration of stress hormones is elevated. If one of these clumps enters a narrowed blood vessel in the heart, the flow of blood may be decreased enough to result in damage to the heart muscle. This may be the primary mechanism when someone experiences stress and has a heart attack.

    Thus, be aware of the importance of keeping the concentration of your stress hormones low in regard to the risk of having a heart attack. If you can keep the concentration of the hormones low you will have a good chance of lowering your risk of having a heart attack. Keeping your stress hormone concentrations low will result in the blood vessels in your heart becoming wider. You should start to do this now, not after you have a heart attack.

5. **THE FUNCTION OF YOUR IMMUNE SYSTEM IS ALTERED**- There are several components to the immune system, which when in balance and functioning properly, help to rid the body of bacteria and viruses. The immune system also makes large concentrations of antibodies when we are immunized, for example, to the flu. The antibodies help to prevent infections. The stress hormones decrease the ability of the immune system to fight off infections and make antibodies. This is why you may notice that when you are experiencing stress the likelihood of developing a cold increases.

My advice is that if you are going for an immunization, for example to the flu or hepatitis or pneumonia, and you are experiencing high levels of stress in your life, you may want to wait until your stress is decreased. The likelihood of making more antibody and be better protected from disease will be increased if you are immunized when you are not under a lot of stress.

Another consequence that occurs when stress hormones change the balance between the different components of the immune system is that **your immune system becomes more capable of reacting to your body** and producing diseases we call 'autoimmune diseases'. Examples of these diseases are psoriasis, multiple sclerosis, rheumatoid arthritis, Crohn's disease, and ulcerative colitis. These diseases tend to get worse when experiencing stress. If you have or know anyone with one of these diseases you know that stress causes these diseases to get worse.

Specific example: Multiple sclerosis:

- Some patients have a type of multiple sclerosis called relapsing-remitting (where there are alternating intervals of disease activity and disease remission). Experiencing a strong stressor predicts an increased risk for the development of lesions in the brain and spinal cord.

- 85% of multiple sclerosis exacerbations in patients with relapsing-remitting disease are preceded by a stressor during the 2 weeks prior to the exacerbation
- Engaging in stress coping behaviors (that reduce the activation of the brain by stress and reduce the elevation of stress hormones) is associated with reduction of disease activity

Using behaviors and techniques that lower the concentration of stress hormones will help to keep the immune system in balance and functioning normally and control the clinical symptoms of these diseases in comparison to when the stress hormones are in high concentration. The frequency of relapse when in remission may also be decreased by keeping stress hormone concentrations low.

6. **THE ABILITY OF YOUR BODY TO HEAL CUTS DECREASES** because the stress hormones interfere with the process of wound healing. When you have a cut or an incision during a surgical procedure, the healing process requires the movement of cells called fibroblasts to the site of the wound. Their ability to get there and to release chemicals that promote closing and healing of the wound is affected by stress hormones. If the hormone concentrations are low, wound healing occurs more quickly.

7. **DIABETES IS MORE DIFFICULT TO MANAGE** because the stress hormones raise the concentration of glucose in the blood. When stress hormones are elevated, hemoglobin A1c (a measure of the average level of blood sugar over several weeks) becomes elevated. This is an indication that glucose is not being well controlled, and the patient is at an increased risk for developing complications associated with diabetes. Using behaviors and techniques to lower the concentration of stress hormones will lower the level of hemoglobin A1c and make glucose management

less difficult with a lowered risk of diabetic complications than when the stress hormones are high.

8. **YOUR WEIGHT IS MORE DIFFICULT TO MANAGE** either because you tend to eat tasty but unhealthy foods high in fats (yes, they may make you feel good) or you don't feel like engaging in physical activities. It is possible that fatty foods act as an antidepressant which contributes to the desire to eat them with resultant weight gain.

9. **TELOMERES SHORTEN**- Telomeres are the protective components (little caps on the ends of your chromosomes) that stabilize the chromosomes. Each time a cell divides the telomeres get shorter. If the telomeres get too short, cells will stop dividing and tissues and organs wear out. Short telomeres have been associated with an increased risk of developing cancer, dementia, and a shorter duration of life.

   Cortisol, one of the stress hormones decreases the activity of an enzyme that restores the length of the telomere. Thus, stress will be associated with shorter telomeres and an increased risk of disease development. Using behaviors and techniques to lower the concentration of stress hormones will be associated with lengthening of telomeres. Obviously, something you do not regularly think about when you think of reasons to increase your ability to cope with stress. However, I want you to be aware of this and, maybe, think about it.

10. **THERE IS AN INCREASE IN THE AMOUNT OF INFLAMMATION IN YOUR BODY**- We are all familiar with the word 'inflammation' because we constantly are encouraged to purchase anti-inflammatory medications for **mild** aches and pains.

    If you have a disease such as rheumatoid arthritis, ulcerative colitis, Crohn's disease, or psoriasis, **strong** inflammation is the reason damage is occurring in the involved tissue. That is why treatment of these diseases involves medications that reduce the amount of inflammation.

However, there are positive aspects to inflammation. When you get a splinter, it is inflammation that identifies the presence of the splinter and brings white blood cells to remove any bacteria that are on the splinter. You know this because the place where the splinter is becomes red, warm, and swollen.

The process of inflammation involves chemical molecules, called cytokines (we have already talked about these molecules as they go to the brain and cause tiredness and getting the 'blues') that are released into the blood.

We now know that stress itself causes cytokines to be elevated in blood, increasing the amount of inflammation that is present. Prolonged stress (chronic stress) may cause a sustained elevation of cytokines in blood. There is accumulating evidence that when continuously elevated, cytokines have a negative effect on health.

The negative effects on inflammation on health include:

- o   Feeling tired all the time
- o   A low level of energy
- o   Moving (walking) slowly
- o   Decreased strength
- o   Feeling weak
- o   A low desire to be physically active
- o   Greater risk of developing a malignancy, heart disease, type 2 diabetes, osteoporosis, dementia

People who live to be over 100 years of age have low levels of inflammation. Maybe that is why they live to be that old.

Individuals who were abused as children have higher levels of inflammation when they are adults and an increased risk of mental and physical health impairment

Lower levels of inflammation are found in individuals who are physically active, socially interactive, joyful, and cope well with stress. These are behaviors that have a positive effect on many aspects of health. A diet containing fruits, vegetables, and nuts also contributes to low levels of the chemicals associated with inflammation. It is important, for long term mental and physical health to keep the amount of inflammation in the body low.

A marker of inflammation that can be determined by a blood test is called C-reactive protein (abbreviated CRP).

People greater than 60 years old who answered YES to these 2 questions had greater levels of inflammation and depression:

- Do you have the feeling that you have not accomplished very much recently?
- Do you feel like giving up?

11. **PAIN PERCEPTION IS INCREASED-** An elevation of stress hormones increases your perception of pain. When stress hormone concentrations are high, aches and pains will hurt more. When stress hormone concentrations are low, pain will hurt less.

An example is the discomfort of delivering a baby. Deep breathing, which you know lowers the concentration of stress hormones, is an important component of the Lamaze program to prepare pregnant women for delivery. The goal is to decrease the concentration of norepinephrine which increases the perception of pain. Less norepinephrine, it is less uncomfortable.

There is an association between pain and emotions with early life abuse increasing the perception of pain. Higher levels of stress and lower levels of optimism increase the perception of pain. Lower levels of stress and higher levels of optimism decrease the perception of pain.

Please remember that engaging in healthy lifestyle behaviors and techniques will have a beneficial effect on many aspects of health, not just a single factor.

If you use the behaviors and techniques you will learn in this journey and you keep the concentration of stress hormones in your body low, the likelihood of your staying healthy as you age will become more likely than if your stress hormones are high. Also remember that the longer you stay healthy as you continue to age will leave less time to develop a chronic disease before you die. Therefore, the goal is to stay healthy, grow older, and then have a short demise. That is the blessing you want to achieve.

How much time have you put into a lifestyle that will help assure that you will be functional and healthy as you age? Probably not as much as the amount of time you have put into worrying about your financial health and activities that provide a rapid pleasurable response. It's time to start thinking about the healthy lifestyle behaviors as pleasurable as they will increase the likelihood of your staying healthy as you age and having a rapid demise. Then, instead of having a fear of growing older, which I'll call gerophobia, you can focus on gerophilia, looking forward to enjoying the health benefits associated with healthy lifestyle behaviors and techniques.

HOW YOU THINK ABOUT YOUR AGE IS SOMETHING I'D LIKE YOU TO USE FOR MOTIVATION TO STAY HEALTHY

One of my favorite quotes is from Satchel Paige because it has important meaning:

"How old would you be if you didn't know how old you were?"

Take your time, think about the significance of what he said.

Research studies show that if you are mentally and physically healthy, the age that you feel you are may be less than your actual (chronological) age. This is what you want for yourself. Of course, the opposite is true if you are not mentally and physically healthy. Then, you may feel older than your chronologic age.

The younger you feel, regardless of your chronologic age, the greater the likelihood you will be mentally and physically healthy as you grow older. As you are becoming aware, the better you cope with stress the greater the likelihood you will be mentally and physically health as you grow older. Thus, if you increase your ability to cope with stress the chance of feeling younger and remaining healthy as you age becomes more likely. Not a bad combination, increasing the likelihood of feeling young and staying healthy while continuing to chronologically age.

Who needs to know their chronologic age? The government, for example, to let you know when you can vote or collect social security. You certainly do not need to know your chronologic age. What is important is how you feel. Chronologic age is not the most important way to consider your age.

In agreement with Satchel Paige I believe that the best way to consider age is the concept of perceived age, how old do you feel you are? It is important because it can have a meaningful effect on your health. Whenever you think about your age I hope you will stop thinking about the number of years old you are as your age.

What does it really mean to be 70? To quote the song "Old Friends" by Simon and Garfunkel, "it's terribly strange". But try telling that to the 80-year-old person who is constantly on the go, running a career, running a home, and being physically active. The active 80-year-old is exercising regularly, laughing a lot, talking about their feelings with friends, and, it is easy to speculate, enjoying life.

Then there's the 80-year-old who has 80 candles on their birthday cake, but who has trouble blowing them out. This person may have difficulty walking because of poor balance, arthritis, or profound mental depression, and may require the care and kindness of others for their most basic human needs. Obviously, the number of years old you are tells you very little about your health and function.

I understand that many of us don't like the idea of growing older. Yet, it's happening to you right now. To that I say, "So What". If you are mentally and physically healthy the number doesn't matter. What matters is how you feel. Increasing your ability to cope with stress will help to reduce the importance of your chronologic age.

I want to present you with an example showing how you think about your age can have an effect on your longevity. I don't want to scare you, I want to use this to motivate you to engage in healthy lifestyle practices.

Your perceived age consists of factors such as how you feel about your physical and mental health, your happiness with your daily life activities, your involvement with others, and your physical limitations.

Please answer the following 2 questions:

1. Do you feel **physically** younger, the same, or older than your chronologic age?
2. Do you feel **mentally** younger, the same, or older than your chronologic age?

Now let's look at some data from a study where people answered the 2 questions.

The study group consisted of 395 men and 770 women age 65-84. The number of deaths over the 13 years after their answering the 2 questions was determined.

The number of deaths over 13 years for perceived **PHYSICAL** age was:

Men: 65 deaths of those whose perceived physical age was **the same** as their actual age

99 deaths of those whose perceived physical age was **older** than their actual age

59 deaths of those whose perceived physical age was **younger** than their actual age

Women: 54 deaths of those whose perceived physical age was **the same** as their actual age

81 deaths of those whose perceived physical age was **older** than their actual age

36 deaths of those whose perceived physical age was **younger** than their actual age

The number of deaths over 13 years for perceived **MENTAL** age was:

Men: 63 deaths of those whose perceived mental age was **the same** as their actual age

139 deaths of those whose perceived mental age was **older** than their actual age

64 deaths of those whose perceived mental age was **younger** than their actual age

Women: 55 deaths of those whose perceived mental age was **the same** as their actual age

82 deaths of those whose perceived mental age was **older** than their actual age

44 deaths of those whose perceived mental age was **younger** than their actual age

The data is clear. Feeling older than one's chronological age increased the risk of mortality even after adjusting for existing diseases. Now go back and look at your answers to the 2 questions.

The bottom line is that you're not going to feel younger than your chronological age if you are not healthy. Increasing your ability to cope with stress will contribute to your staying healthy as you go thru the aging process and your feeling younger than your chronologic age. I hope this is another motivation for you to increase your ability to cope with stress.

Anytime during aging that you start to use healthy lifestyle behaviors you will increase the likelihood of better mental and physical health. Always think of yourself as a functional, active individual who is contributing to the happiness and well-being of others and at the same time receiving happiness from your interaction with others. I know that if you learn to increase your ability to cope with stress, you will increase the likelihood of staying healthy as you continue thru the aging process. That is what you want for yourself.

THERE ARE EVENTS THAT ARE EXPERIENCED EARLY IN LIFE THAT INFLUENCE THE QUALITY OF MENTAL AND PHYSICAL HEALTH THROUGHOUT LIFE

(Maternal stress during pregnancy, childhood abuse, being bullied)

The following is not meant to frighten you. It is meant to make you aware of events that occur early in life that influence both mental and physical health. It is important to know that behavior, learning ability, and mental and physical health are often influenced by aversive experiences that occur early in life.

I cannot over emphasize the importance of this. If future generations are going to be both mentally and physically healthier than our current population, we must find ways to reduce the amount of stress experienced by pregnant women and reduce (eliminate) the abuse of children.

STRESS EXPERIENCED BY A PREGNANT WOMAN

We are currently at an early stage of understanding the fine points of the association between stress experienced by a pregnant woman and its effects on the brain of the fetus. Yes, stress experienced by a pregnant woman may have an effect on the fetus.

Questions can be researched such as whether 1 day of strong stress in the 5th week of pregnancy exerts a similar effect as 3 months of mild stress during the first trimester. Researchers are looking at questions like this.

My feeling is that it doesn't matter. What is important is to reduce the exposure to stress for all individuals, including pregnant women, and to develop and use effective stress coping behaviors and techniques for everyone.

In regard to pregnancy, it is important to reduce stress experienced by a pregnant woman and increase coping skills throughout the 9 months of pregnancy.

Thus, it is important for pregnant women to engage in the behaviors and use the techniques (such as deep breathing and are further described as you continue to read) that will help to keep the concentration of stress hormones low.

There is evidence that stress experienced by a pregnant woman affects learning ability and memory, when the fetus becomes an adult. This may be caused by an alteration of the areas of the brain that are involved with memory and learning.

One of the areas of the brain of the fetus that is affected by a mother's stress is the hippocampus which is also involved in determining whether an individual will experience depression. This may be the reason that children born to mothers who have high levels of stress during pregnancy have an increased risk of developing depression.

To summarize, in humans, a high level of stress hormones in a pregnant woman may reduce birth weight and cause an increased risk of the child having:

- disrupted emotional regulation
- impaired cognitive performance
- decreased brain volume in areas associated with learning and memory
- hypertension, diabetes, heart disease

STRESS BUFFERS DURING PREGNANCY

It is important to know that even if a pregnant woman is experiencing stress in her life, there are buffers which reduce the elevation of stress hormones. Being physically fit and physically active (such as walking) during pregnancy is a buffer. Being in a home where you enjoy being there, is a buffer. Having people to talk to about how you're feeling during your pregnancy is a buffer.

Yes, the effects of stress hormones on the fetus are of concern. However, if a pregnant woman has a lifestyle that reduces the response of the brain to stress there will be less of an elevation of stress hormones and it will be less likely that the fetus will be exposed to high levels of stress hormones.

All pregnant women should engage in the behaviors which help to keep the concentration of stress hormones low. I am not saying this to scare anyone. I am telling you this to encourage pregnant women to use stress coping behaviors during pregnancy. As you continue on this journey you will be provided with many ways to reduce the response of your brain to stress.

THE HARMFUL AND LONG-LASTING EFFECTS OF ABUSE OCCURRING EARLY IN LIFE

Childhood abuse is the improper treatment of a young individual that alters the quality of their mental and/or physical health. Every child (and adult) wants to be warmly held, comforted, made to feel secure, and loved. If they do not feel this way their brain may perceive (have the belief) that they are experiencing stress. If the brain believes it is experiencing stress, there will be an elevation of the concentration of the stress hormones. In young individuals where the brain is still developing and the connections between brain cells are being formed, an elevation of the concentrations of stress hormones may alter the proper development of the brain.

Children who are abused (physically, mentally, sexually, or neglected) are at risk for alteration of their physical and mental health when young and as they age. Often, unfortunately, one or more types of abuse are experienced by a child which increases the risk of mental and physical health problems throughout life.

- Examples of physical abuse are hitting, kicking, shaking, burning, or other use of force that causes pain and/or damage to tissue.
- Examples of mental abuse are verbal abuse that damages a child's self-worth or emotional well-being. Making fun of a child's behavior, telling them they are stupid, causing them to feel shame, withholding affection.
- Examples of sexual abuse are inducing or coercing a child to engage in sexual activities thru coercion or force.
- Examples of neglect are the failure to meet a child's physical or emotional needs thru lack of access to kind and warm parental contact and lack of adequate food, shelter, clothing, social interaction with peers, and medical care.

Of course, not every mental or physical health issue is related to early life abuse. However, many more are than you may have imagined.

Here is an example of the effect of early life abuse on health and longevity. The data is obtained from a study called the Adverse Childhood Experiences (ACEs) study.

Data on health behaviors, health status, and exposure to ACEs were collected from 17,337 adults who were older than 18 years of age during 1995–1997. These were predominantly white middle-class individuals with health insurance. What is important is that they were not from underserved communities where individuals may not have had access to adequate health care resources.

The ACEs included abuse (emotional, physical, and sexual); witnessing domestic violence; parental separation or divorce; and growing up in a household where members were mentally ill, substance abusers, or sent to prison.

The ACE score (count of the number of 'YES' responses to the10 questions listed below) was used as a measure of cumulative exposure to traumatic stress during childhood. The more questions answered with a 'YES', the stronger the association with health issues.

Deaths were identified during follow-up using mortality records obtained from a search of the National Death Index. 1539 people died during follow-up. People with six or more YES answers died nearly 20 years earlier on average than those with NO yes answers (60.6 vs 79.1 years).

In regard to health risk, 9,500 adults who had four or more ACES during childhood had up to 12 times the risk for alcoholism, drug abuse, depression and suicide, with a two- to four-fold increase in smoking and poor self-rated health. Those who experienced adversity as children also had more sex partners and sexually transmitted diseases with higher levels of physical inactivity and severe obesity.

The study also found that ever higher ACE scores progressively increased the risk in adulthood of heart disease, cancer, chronic lung disease, skeletal fractures and liver disease.

Knowing this, I consider it essential that we find ways to reduce the exposure of young children to abuse. I have learned from numerous people who have confidentially spoken to me that abuse crosses all demographic and socioeconomic barriers. This is not just reading about it, this is information from real people who are not part of any study. They talked about the abuse they experienced when young. Many of those who have told me of being abused when young were from upper middle class families. The point is that abuse of children occurs in every segment of our society.

The 10 questions asked in the Adverse childhood Experiences study are listed here. How many do you answer yes to?

1. Did a parent or other adult in the household often or very often... Swear at you, insult you, put you down, or humiliate you? or Act in a way that made you afraid that you might be physically hurt?
   YES_____   NO_____

2. Did a parent or other adult in the household often or very often… Push, grab, slap, or throw something at you? or Ever hit you so hard that you had marks or were injured?

   YES_____ NO_____

3. Did an adult or person at least 5 years older than you ever… Touch or fondle you or have you touch their body in a sexual way? or Attempt or actually have oral, anal, or vaginal intercourse with you?

   YES_____ NO_____

4. Did you often or very often feel that … No one in your family loved you or thought you were important or special? or Your family didn't look out for each other, feel close to each other, or support each other?

   YES_____ NO_____

5. Did you often or very often feel that … You didn't have enough to eat, had to wear dirty clothes, and had no one to protect you? or Your parents were too drunk or high to take care of you or take you to the doctor if you needed it?

   YES_____ NO_____

6. Was a biological parent ever lost to you through divorce, abandonment, or other reason?

   YES_____ NO_____

7. Was your mother or stepmother:
   Often or very often pushed, grabbed, slapped, or had something thrown at her? or Sometimes, often, or very often kicked, bitten, hit with a fist, or hit with something hard? or Ever repeatedly hit over at least a few minutes or threatened with a gun or knife?

   YES_____ NO_____

8. Did you live with anyone who was a problem drinker or alcoholic, or who used street drugs?

   YES_____   NO_____

9. Was a household member depressed or mentally ill, or did a household member attempt suicide?

   YES_____   NO_____

10. Did a household member go to prison?

   YES_____   NO_____

The effects of abuse of a child may not be apparent to an adult. Criticizing the quality of what the child does, comparing the child in a negative way to other children, yelling at the child, confusing the child by having inconsistent behavior toward the child (being warm and loving one day and mean and critical the next), are all perceived by a child as psychological abuse. If the child perceives the event as abuse, the elevation of the stress hormones may alter the normal development of the child's brain. Things to be concerned about are how often the abuse occurs, how long the duration of it is, and how severe it is. Children living in constant fear of the adults who have responsibility for them would be most susceptible to mental and physical health alterations.

ARE THE EFFECTS OF STRESS CAUSED BY ABUSE IN EARLY LIFE REVERSIBLE? That's a very tough question. I don't want anyone who has any of the mental and/or physical health alterations caused by childhood abuse to give up. To say to themselves that there is nothing they can do to improve the quality of their health.

There is something to do! Start using the behaviors and stress coping techniques that I will describe. Keep the concentration of your stress hormones low. When you do this it becomes more likely that you will be developing new connections between the cells of your brain and modifying the negative effects on your health. Be positive. Know that you can start feeling better. Understand why you may have had some of the health effects associated with early life abuse. But now you know that you can improve the quality of your health and life. Sure it takes time. But if you don't try, nothing will happen.

- Read ahead to where I explain 'Expressive Writing' and do it. Do it as often as you wish.
- Read ahead to where I explain 'Meditation' and do it.
- Don't sit around. Be physically active. Get out and walk. Walk often. If there is someone to walk with, walk with them.

Know that you can improve the quality of your health and life!!!!!!

Know that you will benefit by your engaging in the stress coping behaviors and techniques that are being provided to you.

THE HARMFUL AND LONG-LASTING EFFECTS OF BULLYING

Bullying is something that unfortunately, when it is experienced, can have a long-term effect on both mental and physical health. Bullying can be defined as repeated acts involving a real or perceived imbalance of power with the more powerful individual or group abusing those who are less powerful.

Following are long-term effects of being bullied. I provide this information as many people have been bullied and I want to bring awareness to its effects. Being a victim of bullying is something that contributes to making someone who they are.

Please remember that not everyone who is bullied will have effects on their health. The duration and severity of bullying is important. Buffers that reduce the effect of bullying include the caring and warmth of life at home, the support of friends, and the support of teachers.

- Compared to subjects who had never been bullied, those exposed to bullying when in school are at a significantly increased risk of having been diagnosed with depression between the ages 31-51 years. This suggests that the detrimental health effects of bullying early in life may continue into adult life.

- There is an association between bullying by peers when children are approximately 12 years old and the risk of being depressed when 18 years old. Approximately 15% of 18-year olds who had been frequently bullied were depressed while 6% of children who had not been bullied were depressed.

- Being bullied was determined in children between the ages of 7 and 11 years. 27% were occasionally bullied and 15% were frequently bullied. 50 years later the concentration of the markers of inflammation in the blood was compared with those not bullied. The chemicals associated with inflammation were significantly higher in those bullied than not bullied and higher if bullied frequently. Inflammation is associated with an increased risk of poor mental and physical health.

- The prevalence of workplace bullying is approximately 10%. Of course, if you are being bullied at work, it is 100%. Bullying in the workplace can have long term effects on both mental and physical health. The frequency and severity of the bullying may be a factor in whether health is affected. It is important to also consider an individual's life outside of work. An unhappy life outside of work may contribute to the negative health altering effects of bullying at work as the individual has an unhappy life throughout the day. A happy life with little stress may reduce the health effects of being bullied at work.

- Women who were bullied had significantly higher body weight than those not bullied. These findings were not related to parental social class, having emotional problems in childhood, adult social class, smoking, diet, or exercise. Thus, another indication that having been bullied has long term effects on health.

THE EFFECTS OF MULTIPLE TYPES
OF STRESS EARLY IN LIFE

The **long-term** effects of bullying are greater in individuals who have experienced high levels of stress early in life, such as having been abused. Consider that early life abuse has made the brain more susceptible to being affected when the individual experiences stress later in life. We call this being 'sensitized' to stress. Therefore, when bullying occurs later in life in someone who has been abused, the alteration of the function of the brain is greater in comparison to someone who did not have high levels of stress early in life.

Let's now put this together. There are 3 things to consider:

- The level of maternal stress
- Whether abuse occurs
- Whether bullying occurs

CHILD 1	CHILD 2
Low level of maternal stress	High level of maternal stress
Not abused	Abused
Not bullied	Bullied

If you looked at these 2 children it is unlikely that there would be any external differences. Indeed, they would look like 2 normal children. However, we now know that there are important difference in regard to their ability to learn, their behavior, whether they develop depression, their risk of developing heart disease and high blood pressure, their risk of developing diabetes, and even their risk of developing cancer.

What are some of the differences that may be found when comparing these 2 children:

- The DNA in areas of the brain that are involved with behavior, learning and memory may be different. This alteration may affect the structure of the brain, the number of connections between cells of the brain, and the concentration of molecules that enhance communication between brain cells

- Areas of the brain involved with processing of emotions and behavioral regulation are smaller in child 2. Such individuals may be more prone to develop anti-social behaviors. These changes persist into adult life and can influence the development of depression.
- Increased risk of physical health problems when an adult are greater in child 2. Included is a greater likelihood of heart disease, higher blood pressure, diabetes, cancer, and asthma.

My strong view is that we must direct more attention to reducing stress during pregnancy and reducing early life abuse and bullying if we want to have a population (including our children, grandchildren, and great grandchildren) that is mentally and physically healthier than our current population. It doesn't help to pretend that abuse and bullying are not occurring. Its effects are too important to be ignored.

I hope you now realize how important early life is in determining who someone becomes. As you proceed thru this journey and improve your ability to cope with stress it is likely that you will have meaningful health improvements as you continue to age. However, just as importantly you will realize the importance of healthy lifestyle behaviors for all those who you are close to.

I want to repeat this because it is important: Oprah Winfrey, who openly talks about her being physically and sexually abused as a child, asks us to consider when a child has behavioral and learning difficulties to think of what may have happened to that child to make them the way they are. Don't just say they are a bad kid who can't behave but think about what may have happened to the child, what they may have experienced when young, to make them the way they are.

IT IS THE RESPONSIBILITY OF ADULTS
TO HELP CHILDREN MANAGE STRESS
HERE ARE SOME GUIDELINES

- Adults must provide CONSISTENT emotional and physical support

  o It is important to provide an environment where the child does not have to be afraid of what type of behavior the adult will display.
  o The calm behavior must be repetitious so the child will always know that calm and reasonable behavior is the norm.
  o The adult should not show anger toward the child one day and be kind and caring the next.
  o When at home the children should feel safe and secure, get hugged, told they are loved. This behavior should be the same every day.

- Adults must use calming behaviors for themselves to reduce the risk of getting upset by children.

  o Focus on one technique. Deep breathing is what I recommend.
  o The adult may not remember to do deep breathing, so it is always good if someone reminds them, even if the child reminds them. The adult must be accepting of child's advice.

- Children and parents should practice relaxation techniques together.

  o Children should learn to use relaxation techniques when they are calm. If they learn to do relaxation techniques when they are calm, the relaxation effect will be more likely to occur.
  o The relaxation techniques need to be done regularly. Then, when they are under stress they will know what to do and it is more likely to be effective.

I'D LIKE TO MAKE YOU AWARE OF 2 EXPERIMENTAL STUDIES OF THE EFECTS OF STRESS ON THE HEART AND BRAIN

These 2 studies were done in experimental animals. However, the results are worth your being aware of. They provide a dramatic understanding of the importance of increasing your ability to cope with stress for the benefit of your mental and physical health.

The first study was done in monkeys that were living together in the same housing enclosure and eating the same diet. They could eat all the food they wanted. There were many monkeys in the enclosure.

The key points are that (1) they ate the same food and all that they wanted, and, (2) they were living in exactly the same home. The only difference was that some of the monkeys were dominant (they were the bosses) and they abused the monkeys that were passive. The passive monkeys gave in to being pushed around by the dominant monkeys.

When the monkeys passed away the blood vessels of their hearts were studied. The blood vessels from the passive monkeys who were under a lot of stress had considerable atherosclerosis in the blood vessels of their hearts. The blood vessels of the hearts of the dominant monkeys had little atherosclerosis. Thus, the amount of atherosclerosis in the blood vessels of the heart did not relate to diet or housing condition, it related to stress.

The important point is that they were in the same living conditions and ate the same food. Think about the arteries in your heart. Now think about what is important for the development of atherosclerotic heart disease. Diet certainly receives a lot of attention, but now we know (from many studies) that in addition to diet, stress is an important factor for the development of atherosclerotic heart disease. What do you want the arteries in your heart to look like? My message is that if you are using stress coping behaviors and techniques it is wonderful. If not, please start.

The second study was done in rats that either underwent stress or did not. The brains of the rats were then studied and the amount of projections connecting brain cells was determined. The more connections the better the ability to think clearly, remember and learn. There were significant differences in the amount of projections between the brain cells. The amount of projections from the stressed animals were decreased.

What do you want the blood vessels in your heart and your brain cells to look like? I hope these 2 studies motivate you to increase your ability to cope with stress.

BEFORE PROCEEDING LOOK AT THESE INTERESTING QUOTES FROM PEOPLE WHOSE NAME YOU MAY KNOW. I HAVE ADDED THE MEANING I FIND IN THE QUOTE. WHAT DOES IT MEAN TO YOU?

Think about this quote by Pablo Casalas and what it may mean to you:

The man who works and is never bored is never old. Work and interest in worthwhile things are the best remedy for age. Each day I am reborn. Each day I must begin again.

What it means to me: You should find meaningful things (e.g., mental, physical, cultural, educational, volunteer activities, spiritual) that you want to be doing. Things you look forward to doing. It doesn't matter what they are, only that you find them meaningful because they make you feel useful and bring a satisfaction to you. Often, what you find meaningful will provide benefit to another person. If you are not satisfied with what you are doing, try something else. You are never too old to do something new.

Think about this quote by Frederico Fellini and what it may mean to you:

One day I looked into the mirror and thought, "Where did that old man come from?" Then I realized he was me, and all I wanted to do was work.

What it means to me: He is referring to what I call 'cosmetic age'. Sure, we all want to look like we did when we thought we were at our best. However, that is not realistic. Therefore, the age that is more important is our psychologic age- how we feel mentally and physically. If our psychologic age is less than our actual chronologic age the likelihood that we will continue to be mentally and physically healthy as we age becomes more likely. Also, if our work doesn't make us happy when we are older, if possible, it is better to find something else to do.

Think about this quote by Ella Fitzgerald and what it may mean to you:

It isn't where you came from; it's where you're going that counts.

What it means to me: Resiliency (the ability to recover from the effects of aversive early life events) is important. The warmth of a caring relative, or teacher, or member of the clergy, or social group, along with engaging in activities that are meaningful to you and respected by others, help to make where you are going meaningful. If you know of someone who could benefit by having a caring person available to them, it is rewarding if you are that person.

Think about this quote by Mae West and what it may mean to you:

You're never too old to become younger.

What it means to me: To me, being younger means I can be physically active, I smile a lot, I want to keep learning about things I never had a chance to learn about, I feel much younger than my chronological age. I keep thinking about what Satchel Paige said, "How old would you be if you didn't know how old you are". My goal is to continue to age, stay healthy, and have a rapid demise. Do you share this?

NOW I AM GOING TO PROVIDE A DESCRIPTION OF BEHAVIORS, THAT, IF YOU USE THEM, WILL REDUCE THE RESPONSE OF YOUR BRAIN TO STRESS. IN OTHER WORDS,

THEY WILL HELP YOU INCREASE YOUR
ABILITY TO COPE WITH STRESS

Remember: The less activation of the stress reactive brain area when you experience stress, the lower elevation of stress hormones, and as a result stress will have less of an effect on your health.

A way many people have found helpful to remember the stress coping behaviors that are important is to think of the word **RELAX**:

Religion: Enjoying participation in spiritual or religious activities, or simply taking time to reflect on the things that add meaning, purpose, and joy to your life *helps to reduce the negative effect of stress on your health*

Expectations: Being high in optimism, seeing the glass as half full rather than half empty *helps to reduce the negative effect of stress on your health*

Laughter: Having a sense of humor and being able to laugh at some of the things you do *helps to reduce the negative effect of stress on your health*

Acquaintances: Being socially active and spending time with people you enjoy being with *helps to reduce the negative effect of stress on your health*

e**X**ercise: Being physically active (walking as often as you can) and not just sitting around watching television or playing games on a computer **helps to reduce the negative effect of stress on your health**

Let's take a closer look at each of these behaviors and how to increase these behaviors in your daily life (of course you can also figure this out for yourself). Remember, I am not telling you about these so that you can read about them as if they are part of a novel. These are behaviors that can have a significant influence on the quality of your mental and physical health. Please routinely use as many as you are comfortable with. The more you use them the easier it will be to use them as they become part of your life.

RELIGION: INCREASING YOUR PARTICIPATION IN RELIGIOUS ACTIVITIES OR REFLECTING ON AND INCREASING YOUR ENJOYMENT OF ACTIVITIES THAT CALM YOU

- o Religiosity - Being a religious person, enjoying prayer and/or attendance at religious services is associated with an enhanced quality of health and better stress coping ability. Please remember, you must enjoy your participation in religious activities for them to have a positive effect on health. Even if you don't enjoy the religious aspects of religiosity, attendance at religious services and enjoying being there for the social aspects is a wonderful way to increase social interaction.
  - To increase your religiosity:
    - If you find comfort in prayer, make an effort to pray each day.
    - Consider becoming more involved in your religious community and contributing to programs that promote social interaction at your place of worship.
- o Spirituality- I define spirituality as whatever you do and find effective to calm yourself when you are under stress.
  - I do not equate spirituality with religion. I do not believe that you have to be religious to be spiritual.
    - I recognize that this may not be the standard definition of spirituality. However, I believe anything that helps you to be calm is spiritual because it has

a positive effect on the quality of health of the mind and the body.

- You may find spirituality that calms you through listening to pleasing music, reading a book you enjoy, going for a walk, being physically active, spending time with friends, meditating, or seeing beautiful objects in nature. Spirituality is personal and cannot be measured. It is what you find calming and relaxing. Spirituality, which calms the stress reactive brain areas, produces a lowering of stress hormone levels, which enhances the quality of both mental and physical health.

- Reflect on what you may consider to be your own spirituality and what you enjoy doing to relax and calm yourself. Try to increase the amount of time you spend in spiritual activities, especially when you experience stress. The more often you do this, the easier and more effective it will become.

EXPECTATIONS: INCREASING YOUR FEELINGS OF OPTIMISM

o Optimism is the tendency to focus on seeing things in a positive way and by recognizing that even if you do something wrong it doesn't mean you are a bad person. It is OK to make mistakes. Learn from the mistakes you make, but don't dwell on them. Let them go so they don't continually activate the stress reactive areas of your brain. Soon I will teach you the technique I call 'Expressive Writing' that will help you do this.

- Being optimistic is associated with less illness, including heart disease and depression, and more rapid recovery from disease. Those high in optimism may be more likely to have friends, a sense of humor, and be physically active. These traits tend to go together. For example, if you increase the amount of time you are physically active you are likely to feel more optimistic and increase your sense of humor.

- Being higher in optimism is associated with better ability to think and reason as one ages. It is possible that people higher in optimism have lower levels of cortisol (which can damage brain cells) and have lower levels of inflammation (which alters mental and physical health). Thus, seeing the glass as half-full is beneficial for long term mental health.

- To increase your optimism when you are facing one of life's many obstacles:
    - Remember and focus on all the good things that you do throughout the day rather than the negatives. Train yourself to do this by repeatedly thinking of the things that you are proud of. Even if you made a mistake, turn your attention to other things that you are proud of.
    - Each day, if you wish, write about the good things you did and the interactions with others that you enjoyed.
    - Realize that when you are being blamed for not doing well, it is often the person that is unhappy with you that is having the problem.
    - Remember that not being optimistic can have a negative effect on your health.
    - It is OK to make mistakes. Making a mistake does not mean that you are not a good person. Good people make mistakes.

Here is something that I would like you to do. Each morning, before you get out of bed tell yourself something you really like about yourself. Tell yourself something that makes you very special. Get used to doing this. You will be surprised that it does help you to have a positive attitude early in the day and hopefully throughout the day.

LAUGHTER: USING YOUR SENSE OF HUMOR TO CALM YOURSELF

    o   When experiencing stress a sense of humor and being able to laugh helps to keep stress hormone levels low.

- This happens because there are areas of the brain which become active when you think of something funny. These humor responsive brain areas are connected to the stress responsive areas of the brain.
- When the humor responsive areas are activated they decrease the activation of the stress areas and less stress hormones are released.
- An individual with a good sense of humor may not perceive an event as stressful as would someone without or with a low sense of humor.
- Interestingly, individuals with a good sense of humor are usually high in optimism (positive behaviors cluster together). Having a positive outlook and a sense of humor may be excellent stress buffers.

**BEFORE GOING ON I WANT TO PROVIDE
YOU WITH AN EFFECTIVE TECHNIQUE
TO HELP YOU USE HUMOR TO ENHANCE
YOUR ABILITY TO COPE WITH STRESS.
THIS INFORMATION WILL BE PROVIDED
LATER WHEN I GIVE YOU TECHNIQUES TO
COPE WITH ACUTE STRESS. HOWEVER,**

IT IS ALSO APPROPRIATE TO PROVIDE IT HERE, SO YOU CAN START TO USE IT.

The areas of the brain that are activated by humor are linked to the stress reactive areas. When the humor reactive areas are activated they decrease the activity of the stress reactive area.

- However, when you are experiencing stress it is going to be difficult to think of something funny. Therefore, you need to have something readily available, so you don't have to come up with something funny.

- Here's how you do it:

  1. Create an imaginary box in your mind. Leave it plain or decorate it with your imagination.
  2. Now think of some things that you find funny. They can be anything you want, jokes, movies, experiences, family events, etc.
  3. Select 1 or more of these and place it into your imaginary box.
  4. Then when something is upsetting you and causing you stress go to the imaginary box and think about the funny thing you put there. You don't have to say it out loud, just think about it.
  5. As soon as you do this you will decrease the production of stress hormones and feel calm and be able to focus and think clearly.

THE IMPORTANCE OF A SMILE: In addition, since we are talking about humor and feeling good, I want to tell you about a simple technique that is worth considering:

Our facial expressions can have an influence on our brain. The simple act of smiling can increase the positive feeling of joyfulness.

Here's an example that demonstrates this:

1. Scrunch up your face, make the most awful look you can….hold it …now think.. "I am happy"…
2. Were you able to think happy thoughts? Most people are unable to achieve that.
3. Now, let's do the opposite. Put a big happy smile on your face. While holding that smile think of something sad.
4. Is it easy to think of something sad when you have a big smile on your face?
5. Such a simple physical act of just smiling can have an effect on our mind.

Wouldn't it be wonderful to walk around all day with a smile on your face knowing that it will make you feel better and hopefully will have a positive effect on others.

Uh, Oh. You better not because people may ask whether there is something wrong with you because you are always smiling. I wish we could change so it would be normal for people to be smiling more often and hopefully influencing others to do the same.

OK, now let's get back to the important behaviors that will reduce the response of your brain to stress, We have already mentioned 3 behaviors including Religion, Expectations (Optimism) and Laughter.

ACQUAINTANCES: PARTICIPATION IN SOCIAL INTERACTIONS

- Individuals who enjoy (the word enjoy is important) interacting with others, have people they consider as friends, and do not feel lonely, have less stress hormone elevation when they experience stress than individuals who lack social interaction and who feel lonely.
- There are modifying factors that I want you to be aware of:

- • First, there are individuals who are content without a social support system. Even though they do not have people they would call friends, they are not lonely. Indeed, there are people who are more comfortable being alone. What I am saying is that this does not apply to them. The issue is loneliness. If someone is alone and not lonely they are fine.
- • Second, be aware that even if someone is with people they may still be lonely. Just because someone engages in social interactions with others, doesn't mean they may not feel lonely. If you are someone like this your health may be affected in a negative way. Simply stated, we need friends.
- • What is a friend?
  - ▪ Obviously the most important factor is that they also consider you to be a friend. This does not mean acting friendly, but rather wanting to spend time with each other, sharing personal feelings, listening, having patience with each other.
  - ▪ In regard to health benefits of friends it may not be the actual number of people you consider as friends. It may be the number of social contexts that you have where you have friends. What I mean is if, for example, you enjoy being with your family, colleagues at work, congregants at a place of worship, people you play a sport with, people in a club you belong to, you will have an excellent ability to buffer the effects of stress on your brain. This will be much more effective than if the only people you enjoy interacting with are members of your family. The more types of social interaction you have, the more resistant you are to the negative effects of stress on your health.

What do you do if you are lonely and want to increase your social interaction? What I recommend is to encourage the person to become involved in a volunteer activity of something they have an interest in. For example, if they enjoy gardening, consider volunteering at the local botanical garden. If they enjoy reading, volunteer at the local library to read to children. Or become a mentor for students in local schools. Many people enjoy volunteering at a hospital or nursing home. It is important to think of what you would like to do and be bold enough to look for volunteer opportunities in that type of activity.

Of course, someone who is uncomfortable being with people may have difficulty seeking a volunteer position. Even then, there are places you can go to be around people without having to do a lot of talking. For example, go the gym at the YMCA or YWCA and just walk around on a track. You don't have to talk to anyone, just be somewhere other people are.

Individuals who engage in social interactions through marriage, close friends, religious activities, and group associations have lower mortality rates than do individuals without such interactions. Having social support and interactions may contribute to our sense of well-being by adding 'meaning' to life by being wanted and appreciated by others. This helps to keep stress hormones low.

To get a feeling about your level of loneliness how do you answer these following questions? You don't need any sophisticated statistical analysis to get a feeling for your degree of loneliness. How many do you answer in a way that says to you that you are comfortable with and have social interactions:

- I do not feel in tune with the people around me **or** I feel in tune with the people around me
- There is no one I can turn to when I need support **or** I have people to turn to when I need support
- I feel alone **or** I do not feel lonely
- I do not feel part of a group of friends **or** I am part of a group of friends
- I am no longer close to anyone **or** I have close friends
- There are few people I feel close to **or** I have friends I feel close to
- I feel left out **or** I have friends who include me in their activities
- My social relationships are superficial **or** I have meaningful and satisfactory social relationships
- I can't find companionship when I want it **or** companions are readily available to me

Think about your answers. What do they mean to you. Remember, if you are alone and not lonely, it is OK. However, you can be with people and still feel lonely. If I must identify the most important factor that increases the risk of depression, it is loneliness. Perceived social isolation is associated with greater risk of illness and shorter duration of life.

- If you are lonely, when you experience stress, there is more activation of the stress reactive areas of the brain. This causes an elevation in the concentration of stress hormones which have all the effects on mental and physical health that I have been talking about.
- Loneliness increases the risk of developing heart disease (cholesterol deposits in the walls of the blood vessels of the heart) and having a stroke.
- Loneliness and depression are related. Remember, it is possible to be with people and to feel lonely.
- Social support from an individual that one is close to helps the individual maintain engagement in physical activity.

E**X**ERCISE:

There is overwhelming evidence that being physically active (notice that I didn't say 'exercise') decreases the risk of:

- Heart disease including heart attacks and heart failure
- High blood pressure and the risk of having a stroke
- Development of cancer
- Non-insulin dependent diabetes mellitus by helping to keep weight low
- Osteoporosis by strengthening bones
- Obesity by using up calories
- Depression
- Fall-related injuries in older adults by helping to maintain balance while standing and walking

- Functional decline in older adults. This includes both physical activities and mental capacity.
- Sleep problems

This is important!!!! If you have not been physically active it is worthwhile to start to increase your physical activity **REGARDLESS** of your age. Please don't be naive and think that you're ever too old to benefit from engaging in healthy lifestyle behaviors.

It is interesting that mild physical activity activates the same parts of the brain as does stress. It appears that the more times these brain areas are activated by mild physical activity it becomes more difficult for psychologic stress to activate them. Thus, if you are physically active you are likely to have lower concentrations of stress hormones which, as you now know, is associated with a better quality of health.

- It's up to you to engage in physical activities. Don't depend on community programs and the recruitment efforts of others. No one can make you do what you don't want to do. You must want to do it. Get out and get moving. Take the initiative. Do it to increase the likelihood of your staying health as you age.
- Do it regularly, make it a habit. Engage in physical activity each day-if you are able WALK (see list below). After a while you will notice that not being active will make you feel uncomfortable.
- Do what you can do, even if you have aches and pains. A little is better than none.

What do I mean by physical activity? I'll give you a list, but you can and should make up your own. These are just examples and I've included precautions that you not only should be aware of but show that regardless of any physical limitations you have, you can still be physically active. PLEASE NOTE: I AM NOT USING THE WORD EXERCISE, I AM TALKING ABOUTY PHYSICAL ACTIVITY. I do this because people will often say that they don't like to exercise but that they like to be physically active.

EXAMPLES OF PHYSICAL ACTIVITY	EXAMPLES OF ISSUES RELATED TO YOUR HEALTH AND CAPABILITIES
Clean your house	Can you bend over? If so, be careful and only bend as far as you are comfortable. Can you carry a bucket of water? If you have trouble only put as much water in the bucket as you can comfortably carry. If you want to sit on the floor to clean something can you easily stand up? If not, make sure there is something, or someone, to help support you. Do you have arthritis and can't reach over your head? If so, only reach as far as you can. Do you easily get short of breath and have to rest? Fine, cut back when you feel short of breath.
Take a walk (you don't have to walk far or fast-you just have to do it regularly)	Do you have sidewalks that are level? Be concerned about tripping and falling if the sidewalks are not level. You can go to a shopping mall to walk, the zoo, or a local high school track. How far can you walk without getting short of breath or having leg pains? If that occurs, stop or slow down. If you get short of breath is there a place to sit? If you need a bathroom are they accessible? Do you have someone to walk with? It makes it a lot easier to do. If you can't leave your home is there a pathway through your house that you can walk? Don't worry about how long it takes you to do this. Just do it if you are able. If the weather is not good is there a nearby shopping mall you can go to?

Wash your car, or help a friend wash their car	Only do what you can. Somewhat clean is better than not clean.
Stretch to increase your ability to move comfortably and be flexible.	Start slowly. Don't produce pain if you have arthritis. Reduce what you are doing if you have pain. When comfortable resume what you were doing. Having flexibility will help with your balance

THE FOLLOWING BENEFITS OF ENGAGING IN PHYSICAL ACTIVITY SHOULD MOTIVATE YOU TO WANT TO BE PHYSICALLY ACTIVE

- Slowing the rate of muscle loss and keeping bones strong during aging allowing for the maintenance of physical activities.
- Lower blood pressure and risk of a heart attack and often helping to keep cholesterol levels low.
- Better ability to move without pain as one ages, and therefore, more enjoyment of life.
- There is a reduced risk of developing many types of cancer.
- Adults who are physically active are less likely to be depressed than are adults who are sedentary.
- Greater amounts of walking are associated with more cells in the brain and is associated with a reduced risk of cognitive impairment. Physical activity is a non-pharmaceutical intervention to prevent age-related cognitive decline.
- Social support from an individual that one is close to helps the individual maintain engagement in physical activity.
- Lonely people are less physically active than people who are not lonely.

- Children are more likely to have better grades when they are physically fit by engaging in school activities that include physical activity.
- Physical activity done as part of daily activities (for example, house cleaning, walking stairs, going shopping) contributes to staying health as you age

SEXUAL SATISFACTION

Finally, the most difficult behavior to address is sexual satisfaction. Yet, to increase the ability to cope with stress the maintenance of a satisfactory sexual life as one goes through the aging process is important.

Being satisfied with one's sexual life (including activities and frequency) helps to cope with stress. Lack of that satisfaction is a stressor because it is often thought of and associated with disappointment and then depression. As you are well aware, anything that causes activation of the stress reactive brain areas causes an elevation of the stress hormones and an effect on both mental and physical health. Lack of sexual satisfaction and brooding over it will do that.

There is not a single answer that will satisfy all people regarding how to manage the lack of sexual satisfaction if this is an issue for them. This differs for younger vs older individuals. For the older individual lack of a partner (through loss of a spouse or partner through death or going separate ways) and physical changes associated with disease (for example arthritis or heart disease) and concern about one's physical appearance, all can affect sexual desire.

Also, as one ages, what provides satisfaction may change and this may differ for men and women. For example, some older women may be satisfied by having someone to hug, to kiss, or just touch. Other women as they age may want to maintain having sexual intercourse. For men, regardless of age, it seems the most satisfying activity is sexual intercourse or being the recipient of oral sex. Just having someone to hug doesn't seem to be as important for men as it is for women.

Let me state again, "There is not a single answer that will satisfy all people regarding how to manage the lack of sexual satisfaction".

SUMMARY OF STRESS BUFFERING BEHAVIORS

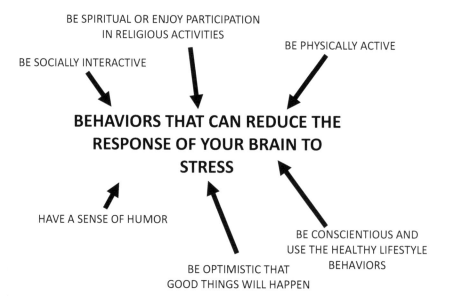

BE SPIRITUAL OR ENJOY PARTICIPATION IN RELIGIOUS ACTIVITIES

BE PHYSICALLY ACTIVE

BE SOCIALLY INTERACTIVE

BEHAVIORS THAT CAN REDUCE THE RESPONSE OF YOUR BRAIN TO STRESS

HAVE A SENSE OF HUMOR

BE CONSCIENTIOUS AND USE THE HEALTHY LIFESTYLE BEHAVIORS

BE OPTIMISTIC THAT GOOD THINGS WILL HAPPEN

REMEMBER: DOING ANY OF THE STRESS COPING BEHAVIORS WILL MAKE IT EASIER FOR YOU TO DO OTHER OF THE BEHAVIORS AND IMPROVE THE QUALITY OF MANY ASPECTS OF YOUR HEALTH

CHANGING BEHAVIOR AND A PLEA

If you currently do not use behaviors that help you increase your ability to cope with stress I am asking you to consider changing your behavior. Please start to include behaviors that help to reduce the activation of the stress reactive areas of your brain. Of course, as I'm sure you know, it is hard to change a behavior that we have been using for many years or decades.

There is a reason why it is hard to change behaviors. We know (and now you know) that our behaviors are defined by the connections between cells of the brain. We also know that the structure of the brain can be changed (we like to say that the brain can be rewired) by events we experience and new things that we learn. This is called 'neuroplasticity', the ability of the brain to transform itself.

When we stop using behaviors that are defined by existing connections between brain cells, the connections eventually come apart so the behavior is unlikely to be used. If we replace that behavior with a new one, the new behavior will be defined by a new pattern of connections between brain cells. This is a difficult process to do effectively. It may take months to occur, requires optimism that one can successfully achieve it, and benefits by social support encouraging staying on the new path and not going back to the old behavior.

My plea to you is that when you are trying to incorporate a healthy lifestyle behavior into your life, be patient. It may take months until that behavior occurs readily when you need to do it. And now you know the reason why. The connections defining the old behavior must come apart and be replaced by the connections defining the new behavior. This may take 6 months. Be patient. Keep using the new behavior as often as you can. Don't only use the behavior when you are experiencing stress, use it when you are doing well. This will help to rewire your brain and make the new behavior easier to remember.

Be optimistic that you will be successful! Ask someone close to you to help you. When they see you are going back to using the behavior you are trying to change they need to remined you of the progress you have made and not to go back!!

Remember, when I mention increasing your ability to cope with stress I am talking about your use of behaviors and techniques (that you will learn as we proceed) that reduce the activation of the areas of your brain that are activated by stress. This results in a reduction of the amount of stress hormones released when your brain perceives something as stress. If the hormones don't go up as much, there is less of an effect on altering your health.

The RELAX behaviors we just learned will help you keep your stress hormone levels low and increase your mental and physical health.

- **R**eligion:
- **E**xpectations:
- **L**aughter:
- **A**cquaintances:
- **X**ercise

Contemplate your strengths and weaknesses with regard to these behaviors.

1. Think of ways to increase these behaviors into your life.
2. Look at your schedule and determine a way to participate in each of these behaviors as often as you can this week and in your future.
3. Write down your long-term goals of why you will benefit by increasing your use of these behaviors and how you are going to achieve your goals.

WE CANNOT MAKE THE STRESS IN YOUR LIFE GO AWAY but we can change the way your brain responds to stress. By being better able to cope with stress you will have less of an elevation of stress hormones. It is the elevation of the stress hormones that alters your mental and physical health.

Be aware that not all of the material that we are providing may work for you. Everyone is different. Not everyone likes modern art, or a New York strip steak, or Sushi. All we can do is hope you find the information life changing so that as a result you will not only achieve a better quality of mental and physical health but by becoming a role model for healthy lifestyles you will also help others to achieve the same.

For motivation, let's review the health benefits again because it is important to remember the health benefits of increasing your ability to cope with stress. When you keep your stress hormones low by coping with stress, each of the health factors listed below improves. As is clear, the quality of both mental and physical health gets better:

- You have less difficulty thinking clearly and focusing
- You are less likely to act impulsively
- You will be less likely to become depressed and have the 'blues'
- Your ability to remember things will increase
- Your heart will beat less rapidly
- Blood pressure will be lower
- There is less accumulation of cholesterol into the blood vessels of the heart reducing the risk of having a heart attack
- Blood platelets will not stick to each other reducing the risk of having a heart attack
- The function of the immune system is improved
- The ability of the body to heal wounds increases
- Diabetes is easier to manage
- Weight is easier to manage
- Telomeres on the ends of your chromosomes become longer and are associated with better health
- The amount of inflammation in the body decreases

Look at the list again; everything on it is a meaningful factor in the quality of your mental and physical health. Also remember that children learn their behaviors from those they love. Make sure you are a meaningful role model for the children who are important to you. Your use of healthy lifestyle behaviors will be meaningful to them as they see you are happy and healthy.

Before going on I want you to look at this information regarding modification of the risk of developing cancer as related to using healthy lifestyle behaviors:

This is a study of 130,000 Caucasians. 28,000 used healthy behaviors. Without question, many cancers can be prevented by using healthy lifestyle behaviors.

Healthy Behaviors Had approximately 40% FEWER cancers and cancer deaths than those with unhealthy behaviors	Unhealthy Behaviors Are
Never smoked or smoked in past	Smoking
No or moderate alcohol drinking	Uses alcohol regularly
BMI 18.5-27.5	Obese, BMI>30
Vigorous physical activity of 75-150 minutes/week	Sedentary

If smoking is removed then approximately 20 % of cancers are associated with unhealthy lifestyles. The unhealthy lifestyles associated with cancer (other than smoking) are:

- Lack of physical activity
- An unhealthy diet high in saturated fats (meats) and low in fruits, vegetables, nuts, and fiber
- Excess alcohol intake (1 drink a day is OK)
- Obesity (a BMI greater than 30)

BEFORE PROCEEDING LOOK AT THESE QUOTES FROM PEOPLE WHOSE NAME YOU MAY KNOW. I HAVE ADDED THE MEANING I FIND IN THE QUOTE. WHAT DOES IT MEAN TO YOU?

Think about this quote by Bernard Baruch and how it may relate to you:

To me, old age is always fifteen years older than I am.

What it means to me: Again, one of my favorite and meaningful quotes is from Satchel Paige, "How old would you be if you didn't know how old you are". The quote applies to what Bernard Baruch said.

Think about this quote by Dorothea Kent and how it may relate to you:

A man ninety years old was asked to what he attributed his longevity. "I reckon," he said, with a twinkle in his eye, "it's because most nights I went to bed and slept when I should have sat up and worried."

What it means to me: It is important to learn to let go. Don't continuously think about the things you cannot fix or change. They are over. Continuing to think about things that caused you stress in the past, will continue to activate your stress reactive brain areas. Focus on the good things in your life. When you are young make sure you have done things that you are proud of and that you can think about when you are older. Of course, there will be things that you have experienced that are difficult to forget. But try to make sure that you have things to divert your attention to that put a smile on your face. If needed you can use the technique of expressive writing that is described in the section discussing chronic stress.

Think about this quote by Ann Landers and how it may relate to you:

Inside every seventy-year-old is a thirty-year-old asking, "What happened?"

What it means to me: Cosmetic age is how we look to yourself when we look in the mirror. How much does it matter if we feel mentally and physically younger than our chronologic age? It is how we feel rather than how we look that is important. Of course, how we look may make us feel sad. Then, the focus should be from Satchel Paige, "How old would you be if you didn't know how old you are", and hopefully, appearance will not be a major part of that decision.

Think about this quote by Albert Einstein and how it may relate to you:

The ideals which have lighted me on my way and time after time given me new courage to face life cheerfully have been Truth, Goodness, and Beauty.

What it means to me: Don't be cynical, don't be hostile, be kind, be considerate, smile a lot, enjoy being with people, do good things that others appreciate. No one wants to spend time with someone low in optimism, without a sense of humor, and only focusing on themselves. Hope you don't have to look back and regret things you did or said that have caused discomfort for others. A beautiful life is one filled with kindness and doing things for others.

NOW LET'S GET BACK TO LEARNING TO COPE WITH STRESS

THE FOLLOWING PROVIDES TECHNIQUES FOR YOU TO USE THAT WILL INCREASE YOUR ABILITY TO COPE WITH ACUTE STRESS

THE 3 TECHNIIQUES ARE DEEP BREATHING, THE USE OF HUMOR, THE USE OF A CHANT

ACUTE STRESS occurs suddenly when you don't expect it and has a short duration

From what you have read you know when you experience stress there is a rapid elevation in the concentration of stress hormones that makes it difficult for you to focus and to think clearly. The problem is that when you experience acute stress you will have difficulty remembering to use one of the techniques that will lower the concentration of your stress hormones.

Therefore, there is more to it than just learning the techniques. You must remember to use them. Remember, as has been explained above, that it may take as long as 6 months to stop using a behavior and replace it with a new behavior. Be patient but be persistent in wanting to use healthy lifestyle behaviors.

To help you remember to use a technique that rapidly lowers the concentration of stress hormones:

- Share this information about using the stress coping techniques with family, friends, and colleagues. When they see you are upset about something they can remind you to calm yourself and when you see they are upset, you can remind them to do the same.
- Another thing you can do is to put sticky notes everywhere you may be with messages reminding you to use one of the techniques

I want to point out that not everyone responds to acute stress in the same way. Some show little change of behavior when experiencing acute stress and others may go into a rage reaction. The difference of how one responds to acute stress is likely due to one of the following:

- how much stress the individual experienced when they were young
- how long a time, frequency, and effectively they have been using the stress coping techniques
- how happy they are at the time of experiencing the stress
- whether they are alone or with people they enjoy being with

It is important to remember that individuals who have high levels of stress early in life may become sensitized to stress. This means that when they experience stress later in life they may react more rapidly with a higher level of stress hormones being released. This may cause them to lose control and even have a rage reaction. When this occurs remember that the rage is usually a reflection of what the individual experienced when they were young. It is due to what was done to them. This is a good reason why we must do all we can to reduce the amount of high levels of stress children experience.

I'M GOING TO REPEAT THE METHOD FOR DEEP BREATHING THAT WAS PROVIDED TO

**YOU EARLIER. I'D RATHER DO THIS HERE
THAN REFER YOU TO THE PREVIOUS PAGE.**

**COPING WITH ACUTE STRESS:
DEEP BREATHING FOR CALMING YOURSELF
WHEN EXPERIENCING AN ACUTE STRESSOR**

Deep breathing is a technique that you will be able to use to calm your mind, reduce the concentration of stress hormones in your blood, and contribute to an enhancement of your health. Deep breathing is the technique for coping with acute stress that many people use.

What is deep breathing?

When we experience stress or something unexpected happens we often hold our breath or decrease how deeply we inhale. When we do this carbon dioxide increases in our blood and causes the brain to release a stress hormone that interferes with our ability to think clearly. The hormone is called 'norepinephrine'. Getting more oxygen into your blood by breathing deeper will decrease the amount of stress hormone released.

Deep breathing is exactly what it says. Take a deep breath to get more air into your lungs which will allow more oxygen to enter your blood. When you increase the amount of oxygen in your blood, your brain will detect the increased oxygen and will respond by decreasing the concentration of stress hormones in the blood.

Use the following to learn how to increase the volume of air flowing into the lungs. The essential point is that by pushing the wall of your abdomen out, your diaphragm will drop, increasing the space that the lungs can expand into. This maximizes the flow of air into the lungs and of oxygen into the blood.

DEEP BREATHING INSTRUCTIONS :

1. Take a deeper inhalation than usual. To do this you must push the wall of your abdomen out as you breathe in and returning as you exhale and push the air out.
2. Breathe through your nose or mouth. Whichever is more comfortable.
3. Do not take more than five deep breaths. If you feel a little dizzy, take fewer deep breaths. Usually you will feel calm and thinking clearly before taking 5 deep breaths.
4. If you still feel that you need to do more wait 15 minutes before doing it again. However, it is unlikely you will have to repeat it.
5. Do not feel that you must take 5 deep breaths. Often 2 or 3 is sufficient to produce relaxation allowing you to be calm and to think clearly.

It is important to emphasize that you should PRACTICE this technique when you are calm and relaxed to increase your ability to do it when needed. It is hard to do a relaxation technique without practicing it. So please practice when you are calm. Then it is there for your use when you need it. You will become more efficient in your everyday life and better equipped to deal with life's stresses and challenges when you keep the concentration of your stress hormones low.

- Please remember: When your mind perceives something as stress it is difficult to think clearly. Thus, you may not remember to take 3-5 deep breaths.
- Therefore, remember to share this technique with your family and friends. When they see that you are upset they can remind you to deep breath and when you see that they are upset you can remind them.

POSTURE AND BREATHING

As I've just discussed, increasing the amount of air that flows into your lungs when you breathe in, can have an effect on lowering the concentration of stress hormones. Therefore, it makes sense to maximize the flow of air into your lungs. An excellent way to do this is to have an upright posture. What I do is try to remember, as often as possible, to squeeze my shoulder blades together. That helps me to stand upright and increases the volume of air that can flow into my lungs when I inhale.

Take your time, there is no hurry, spend as much time as you like on this section, the goal is to learn and increase your ability to cope with stress, don't cause stress for yourself, patience and repetition will benefit you

Remember this: We cannot make the stress in your life go away but we can change the way your brain responds to stress. By being better able to cope with stress you will have less of an elevation of stress hormones. It is the elevation of the stress hormones that alters your mental and physical health.

Testimonials about deep breathing from people who have participated in our stress coping program:

- As soon as I feel stressed, I think oh I need to belly breathe and I do and instantly it helps to calm me.
- I give credit to my class for saving my relationship at home. It is amazing how important it is to breathe and walk away from a situation when one gets really angry and hurt.
- I have already experienced relief physically and emotionally from changes in my breathing alone.
- I am able to breathe when I get upset and not respond so quickly without thinking
- This past week I had a hospital procedure, as I lay on the operating table I was feeling anxious. Automatically I began to breathe and visualize. The procedure was done before I knew it and I realized how effective and useful the techniques I learned were.
- The littlest things would stress me out and I would say things that I really didn't want to say out loud and I use to be very impatient. I

have learned to be way more laid back and to walk away and take a couple deep breaths

- Benefits that I've experienced: much less aggressive driving; less bothered by rush hour traffic; able to be calmer in interactions with others; better listener; able through deep breathing to reduce post-surgical back pain; and improved sleep.
- Just taking a few seconds to do something as easy as "breathing" can make such a difference in your day to ease the stressors. I also find myself enjoying the "moment" more often, taking the time to appreciate situations that are very important in my life.
- I have taken the knowledge I received and have taught it to my husband who was very reluctant at first, but now I see him taking a few seconds to breathe before he deals with difficult situations, I even got him to "Write"
- Learning to breathe has helped me with stressful situations at home and at work.
- I find myself continually using the deep breathing technique to get me through excessively busy times
- I forget to just breathe at times, and I didn't realize the impact this had on my health. I am now focusing on my breathing, which I needed with a busy schedule and the demands of a 10 month old baby.

COPING WITH ACUTE STRESS: HUMOR THIS WAS PRESENTED EARLIER BUT I AM REPEATING IT HERE IN THE SECTION ON TECHNIQUES TO COPE WITH ACUTE STRESS

Another way to rapidly become calm and lower the concentration of stress hormones when experiencing an acute stressor is to find something you consider funny. Humor will reduce the production of the stress hormones. I mentioned this earlier and now I want to give you a way to activate the humor responsive areas of your brain. Also remember to smile. The more time I spend smiling when out for a walk, the easier and more comfortable it is to do.

The explanation for the benefits of humor are that the areas of the brain that are activated by humor are linked to the stress reactive areas. When the humor reactive areas are activated they decrease the activity of the stress reactive area.

- Of course, when you are stressed it is difficult to think of something funny, so it is a good idea to have something ready.
- Therefore, you need to have something readily available, so you don't have to come up with something funny.
- Here's how you do it:

  1. Create an imaginary box in your mind. Leave it plain or decorate it with your imagination.
  2. Now think of some things that you find funny. They can be anything you want, jokes, movies, experiences, family events, etc.
  3. Select 1 or more of these and place it into your imaginary box.
  4. Then when something is upsetting you and causing you stress go to the imaginary box and think about the funny thing you put there. You don't have to say it out loud, just think about it.
  5. As soon as you do this you will decrease the production of stress hormones and feel calm and be able to focus and think clearly.

Try this technique often. It is easy to do and has the biologic mechanism described above.

Remember, it will be difficult to think of something funny when you are upset. That is why it is important to already have the funny thought you will use stored away ahead of time. It will be there when you need it.

COPING WITH ACUTE STRESS: CHANTING

Another technique that is effective to help reduce the response of the brain to an acute stress is to train your brain to associate a few words with your being calm. This is known as a Pavlovian conditioned response. Dr. Pavlov rang a bell when he fed dogs. After several times doing this the dogs associated the sound of the bell with being fed. Then, when the dogs heard the sound of the bell their stomachs reacted as if they had actually been fed.

Train your mind to associate a pleasant short phrase with the times you are calm. When you are stressed, thinking the phrase to yourself will cause the brain to decrease the concentration of stress hormones.

This is how you can use this conditioning response to reduce the production of stress hormones when you experience an acute stressor.

- Select the phrase or word you will use. If you wish you can set them to a simple tune, one that you find pleasant or one that has a religious feeling to it, such as the tune of a Gregorian chant. If you don't want to use a tune, don't.
- Some examples are: "I am a good person", or, "All will be well", or "I will be well", or just "calm". You decide what word phrase you want to use.
- Practice this for several days, thinking your word or chant to yourself when you are calm and relaxed. You want your mind to associate the word or chant with your being calm and relaxed.
- When you think your word or chant to yourself while you are calm, you are training your brain to associate the word or chant with being calm. That is why you have to think it many times on many days when you are calm. Your brain will learn that when your mind thinks the word or chant it means it is time for the brain to calm down.
- Your brain will then drop the concentrations of stress hormones and you will, indeed, feel calm.

You have now learned about 3 ways you can rapidly calm your brain and lower the concentration of stress hormones. At different times when you experience stress you may decide to take a few deep breaths, go to your use of humor, or think your chant. All may be effective for you, or just one or two of them may be effective. Decide what works best for you. Use what is effective for you to calm yourself.

If you want to know what most people use, it is the deep breathing technique

PLEASE REMEMBER

- When you need to use one of the three techniques to calm yourself after experiencing acute stress, YOU MAY NOT REMEMBER TO DO IT.
- Acute stress interferes with your ability to think clearly and to focus.
- 2 hours later you will suddenly remember that you should have taken 3-5 deep breaths, or used humor, or use your chant.
- That is why it is so important to share this information with family, friends, and colleagues.
- When they see you upset about something they can remind you to calm yourself and when you see they are upset, you can remind them to do the same.

Take your time, there is no hurry, spend as much time as you like learning to cope with acute stress. The goal is to learn and increase your ability to cope with stress. Don't cause stress for yourself, patience and repetition will benefit you

Remember this: We cannot make the stress in your life go away but we can change the way your brain responds to stress. By being better able to cope with stress you will have less of an elevation of stress hormones. It is the elevation of the stress hormones that alters your mental and physical health.

ACUTE VS CHRONIC STRESS

What is the difference between acute and chronic stress?

ACUTE STRESS is unanticipated, has a sudden onset, and is of a **short duration**. It usually ends after a short time because the event causing the stress is no longer present. The 3 techniques to rapidly lower the concentration of stress hormones when you experience acute stress have just been explained. They include deep breathing, the use of humor, or the use of a chant.

CHRONIC STRESS however, is what it says it is. **IT IS CHRONIC.** It is there for a long time and while your brain is perceiving whatever it is as causing stress, the stress reactive brain areas are active and the stress hormones are elevated **AFFECTING YOUR MENTAL AND PHYSICAL HEALTH.**

It is important to understand that our brain will only consider something as stress if our brain perceives it as stress. This has 2 aspects:

1. Your brain must believe that whatever the event is, is stress. Your brain may do this because, for example, (a) you have previously experienced the event and it caused you stress, (b) you don't understand why the event is happening and you are frightened, (c) you think the event will cause you to do something inappropriate, (d) it is physically painful.

2. You think of the event as stress, even if at the time it may not actually be something that is causing stress. This is important because of the difference between stress and anxiety.
    a. Stress is real; it is something you have to deal with.
    b. Anxiety is in your imagination. Whatever caused the stress is over. However, you keep thinking about it. "Why did I do what I did", "I should have done it in a different way", "I embarrassed myself". The point is that it's over; we all need to learn to let things go when they are over. If not, because we keep thinking about

it we will keep activating the stress reactive brain areas and that will have an effect on our health.

c. Mark Twain knew about this. He said, "I'm an old man and I've known a great many troubles, but most of them never happened". He is telling us that 'anxiety' often has more to do with imagination than reality.

TECHNIQUES FOR COPING WITH CHRONIC STRESS

Now let's direct attention to reducing the effect of chronic stress on our mental and physical health. Chronic stress is any aspect of your daily life that activates the stress reactive areas of your brain. As you now know, when that happens there is an increase in the concentration of several hormones that alters your mental and physical health.

EXPRESSIVE WRITING: A TECHNIQUE FOR COPING WITH CHRONIC STRESS

Anxiety is continually thinking about things, for example, that you didn't do well, and you are upset about. However, it happened in the past. By continuing to think about it you keep the stress reactive brain areas active and the stress hormones high. Obviously, we don't want to keep thinking about things that are over, that we can't do anything about. Therefore, it would be good to be able to forgive others for things they did that upset you and to forgive yourself for mistakes you made and are still stewing about. Not easy to do but I recommend using the following technique of Expressive Writing to do this

Interestingly, writing can contribute to the prevention of illness and help you move ahead by reducing the anxiety associated with things that are of concern to you. The writing technique that I am going to ask you to use is different than keeping a daily diary, often called "Journaling". When you keep a Journal you may write about the things that happen to you or that you find meaningful. You may keep your journal so you can refer to it again. However, someone may find your journal meaning that there are things you would rather not put into your journal. If you would like to keep a daily Journal, please do so. However, in addition, please consider doing the following writing technique called, 'Expressive Writing'.

Expressive writing helps to let go of those things that cause you anxiety but are no longer events that are real but are still in your mind. We need to be able to let go of the things that are over and to learn from them. The technique of Expressive Writing is very helpful for this.

You can use Expressive Writing to write about things that have bothered you for years or something that occurred yesterday and is bothering you. It is simple to do. However, the beneficial effects are usually dramatic.

- Expressive Writing allows you to write about your most private, personal, and intimate issues.
- Expressive Writing allows you to write about the things you cannot discuss with anyone.
- Expressive Writing allows you to write about the things you do not want anyone to judge you about.
- Don't be afraid to write about highly personal and private issues.
- Nobody will ever see what you write. After you finish doing Expressive Writing you will tear the paper into small pieces and flush it away:

Whatever you write about will not go away from your mind. However, you will have the feeling of it becoming less meaningful, less recurrent, and less stress or anxiety producing. You will be calmer. You may notice that you are sleeping better and having the 'blues' less often.

While doing expressive writing you may cry or even start to sob. It is normal, don't worry about it.

EXPRESSIVE WRITING DIRECTIONS :

Take a sheet of paper and something to write with. You cannot use a keyboard, you must write. Find a quiet place where you will not be disturbed for 15 minutes:

- Pick any issue of concern to you to write about
- The only rule is that you write continuously for 15 minutes. If you run out of things to write about, just repeat what you have already written. Don't worry about grammar, spelling, or sentence structure.
- While writing DO NOT READ what you have already written.
- **When you finish writing, tear up what you have written without reading it and flush it away**
- **No one will ever see what you wrote.**
- Write as often as you want to. If you find it helpful, and I believe you will, keep doing it. Why would you want to stop.

Why does this work?

The answer is that we don't know. It doesn't matter that we don't know. It just works.

AN ADDITIONAL WRITING EXERCISE YOU MAY WANT TO TRY:

Whenever you wish, write about something you are grateful for. It may be as few or many words as you want.

Do not throw this away, keep it. Then whenever you are feeling "blue", refer to some of the things that you are grateful for.

GUIDED IMAGERY: A TECHNIQUE FOR
COPING WITH CHRONIC STRESS

Guided imagery is something that you listen to that uses your imagination to create beautiful and comfortable thoughts and pictures in your mind. Where the temperature, smell, sounds, people, sights, are defined by you and therefore you select what you find beautiful and relaxing. It's calming for you because you create what you want to be beautiful and calming.

When you are listening to guided imagery the thoughts that are disturbing to you are set aside as you direct your attention to the imaginary world you create for yourself. This allows the stress reactive areas of your brain to become calm and the concentration of stress hormones to decrease.

The more you listen to Guided Imagery, the more effective it becomes. Your brain will become conditioned to calm down when you think of the guided imagery, just as with conditioning your brain to a chant. If you listen often, when you are calm and happy, and then think about it when you are upset, your brain will quickly take you back to a state of calmness.

You can listen to our Guided Imagery at:

- healthylifestyle.podbean.com
- First please listen to the track labeled "MENTAL JOURNEY"

If you prefer, rather than listening to a guided imagery you can read the following to yourself (or have someone read it to you) and practice it. Do this slowly. Read each line and pause for as long as you like. It can be for 5 seconds or 5 minutes. You decide. After a while all you will have to do is think about it and you will decrease the activity of the stress reactive brain areas:

- Breathe slowly and deeply.
- Think of an ideal place that you find peaceful and relaxing. It doesn't have to be real. Make it the most relaxing place you can imagine.

- When you are in that place leave any worries or concerns behind.
- For a short time don't be concerned about them.
- Focus on the peacefulness that you experience in this special place you have created for yourself. While you are in this imaginary place there is nothing you are going to do to address the things that worry you, so find a few minutes not thinking about them.
- When you are ready put a smile on your face and think how lucky you are to be engaging in behaviors and techniques that are contributing to improving and maintaining your health.

Take your time, there is no hurry, spend as much time as you like on learning and practicing. The goal is to learn and increase your ability to cope with stress, don't cause stress for yourself. Patience and repetition will benefit you.

REMEMBER THIS: We cannot make the stress in your life go away but we can change the way your brain responds to stress. By being better able to cope with stress you will have less of an elevation of stress hormones. It is the elevation of the stress hormones that alters your mental and physical health.

MEDITATION: A TECHNIQUE(S) FOR COPING WITH CHRONIC STRESS

Meditation is another technique you can use to increase your ability for coping with stress. If you want, you can go onto the Internet and find many different types of meditation with names such as Transcendental Meditation, Qi Gong, Mindfulness, and Zen Meditation. However, please pay attention to what I am providing.

BEFORE PROCEEDING YOU NEED TO HAVE AN UNDERSTANDING OF THE PURPOSE OF MEDITATION

Meditation is a technique to focus your attention on something that has no emotional meaning to you. If you are not thinking about things that cause you stress, the stress reactive areas of your brain will calm down. When they are calm the concentration of stress hormones decreases and many aspects of health increase as I constantly am describing.

Personally, I don't care what technique is used to achieve this goal. What is important is that you have something that works for you and a way to calm the stress reactive areas of your brain and lower the concentration of stress hormones. If you want to do this with meditation, fine. If you find other techniques work better for you, do them. It's up to you. I am providing you with options.

Meditation is similar to Guided Imagery but in Guided Imagery you have something to listen to (healthylifestyle.podbean.com). With meditation you use your mind to produce calmness and relaxation. You don't listen to something.

The goal of meditation is to find a way for you to **NOT** pay attention to thoughts that may activate the stress pathways in your brain. Indeed, that is the goal of all stress coping techniques and by now you understand why.

You probably will not learn to do this quickly. You must practice and repeat all of the techniques being taught to you. If you have taken piano lessons, you know that without practice your mind could not get your fingers to where you wanted them to be. Your mind gets better with practice. The more you practice relaxing your mind, the easier and more effective it will become.

I am going to explain a simple meditation technique that you can use. Just like everything else you are learning, it may or may not work for you. If it doesn't use the other techniques that you have learned or make up your own meditation. The main thing that is important is that you make a commitment to work to achieve a better quality of mental and physical health for yourself so you become a role model for those who are important to you.

As with all of the stress coping techniques, the more you use it the more effective it becomes. Also remember to practice the techniques when you are calm and relaxed so it will be easier to use when you are experiencing stress.

WILL MEDITATION HELP WITH ANXIETY?

The answer is yes. When you are dealing with an issue that causes you anxiety, being able to not think about it by doing a meditation is helpful for calming the stress reactive brain areas. If there are issues that are causing you anxiety, I recommend doing the Expressive Writing technique.

- Remember, stress is real; it is something we have to deal with.
- Anxiety is in our imagination. Whatever caused stress is over. However, we keep thinking about it.

"Why did I do what I did", "I should have done it in a different way", "I embarrassed myself". The point is that it's over; we need to learn to let things go when they are over. If not, we will keep activating the stress reactive brain areas and have an effect on our health.

MEDITATION TECHNIQUE: Below is the basis of a simple meditation technique for you to read and practice. Of course, once you get the idea of what you need to do, you may wish to and should make up your own meditations.

Remember, all you are trying to do is **NOT** think about things that may activate the stress reactive areas of the brain. Think about something that makes you happy. Smile while thinking about it. When you are not thinking about something that upsets you, the stress reactive areas of your brain will calm down.

- Do this in a place that is quiet and private so that you are not disturbed by noise or people.
- Select a word that you will use as a focus of your attention. The word should not have any meaning to you. Some examples are CALM or PEACE or RELAX. You can also choose your own.
- Focus your attention on your breath as you breath in and out. You already know that this will help you to be calm and to think clearly. Say the word to yourself each time you exhale.
- Remember, that meditation is a trick that for a few minutes allows you to focus on a neutral event rather than thoughts that activate the stress reactive areas of your brain. Knowing that there is nothing that you are going to do about the thought that is disturbing you for the brief time that you are meditating, will help you not to think about it.
- The importance of the word and paying attention to your breathing is to get your attention away from the thoughts that are disturbing to you.
- Sit, be comfortable, you can close your eyes or leave them open, whatever you prefer.
- Meditate only do so as long as you are comfortable doing it. Even 2-3 minutes is better than not at all.
- That's it. Just do it and practice. Remember, the more you practice something, the easier it becomes to do it and the more effective it becomes. Practice when you are calm.
- The more you practice the easier it will become for you to not think about the things that are bothering you.
- Even 30 seconds can be effective once your brain has become conditioned to associating when you are meditating with being calm.
- Stop when you feel it is time to stop. You decide.
- **Don't meditate while driving.**

It may take several weeks before you begin to feel comfortable with meditation and realize that the technique is helping you to feel calm. Don't give up by being disappointed if you do not feel that the technique is working for you after your first or second try. Keep at it.

Always Remember: Learning to relax will not make you a less effective person or negatively affect your work performance. In fact, learning to relax will make you more efficient in your everyday life, increase your feeling of being calm, and will enable you to interact better with others.

> **Take your time, there is no hurry, spend as much time as you like learning this technique. The goal is to learn and increase your ability to cope with stress, don't cause stress for yourself, patience and repetition will benefit you:**

REMEMBER THIS: We cannot make the stress in your life go away but we can change the way your brain responds to stress. By being better able to cope with stress you will have less of an elevation of stress hormones. It is the elevation of the stress hormones that alters your mental and physical health.

THE IMPORTANCE OF A SMILE (I told you about this earlier when I talked about the importance of a sense of humor-but I want to remind you)

- Our facial expressions can have an influence on our brain.
- The simple act of smiling can increase the positive feeling of joyfulness.
- Here's an example:
- Scrunch up your face, make the most awful look you can….hold it …now think.. "I am happy"…
- Were you able to think happy thoughts? Most people are unable to achieve that.
- Now, let's do the opposite. Put a big happy smile on your face. While holding that smile think of something sad.
- Is it easy to think of something sad when you have a big smile on your face?
- Such a simple physical act of just smiling can have an effect on our mind.
- Wouldn't it be wonderful to walk around all day with a smile on your face.

Uh, Oh. You better not because people may ask whether there is something wrong with you because you are always smiling. I wish we could change that so it would be normal for people to be smiling more often and hopefully influencing others to do the same.

ANOTHER TECHNIQUE THAT YOU MAY FIND HELPFUL IS CALLED 'PROGRESSIVE MUSCLE RELAXATION'

I would recommend using this technique when things are bothering you and instead of using your mind to calm yourself you feel like doing something physical. For example, you may want to go for a walk, or clean your house, or mow the lawn. The technique of Progressive Muscle Relaxation involves contracting and then relaxing muscles starting at your head and working your way down your body.

Receiving benefit from this technique may take some practice. Therefore, don't do it just once and give up. Try it several times. You will be able to develop your own way to do Progressive Muscle relaxation, I am just providing you with an example I find helpful.

- Begin by sitting comfortably in a chair and taking 2-3 deep breaths. You already know that you will start to feel relaxed
- What you will now do is tense and relax different muscles. As a general rule you tense for about 5 seconds and then relax for about 30 seconds before tensing again. Remember, this is a general rule. You can use your own timing. Don't be concerned about being exact with the timing.
- Start by making small circles with your head in one direction and then the other. Do 2-3 in each direction. If it hurts your neck, don't do this.
- Next, extend your arms in front of you at a height that is comfortable for you, with your palms up. You can rest them on your legs if it makes it easier.
- Now clench your fists and tighten the muscles in your upper and lower arms. Hold it for about 5 seconds (don't create stress

for yourself by worrying about how long 5 seconds is-just be approximate). Then relax for about 30 seconds (again, don't worry about whether its 15 or 45 seconds) and do it again, only if you are comfortable doing it again.

- Now take 2-3 deep breaths to relax.
- Now tense the muscles of your forehead, eyes, and chin. If you think someone will laugh at your expression, make sure no one is around. Do this 2-3 times.
- Shrug your shoulders, hold it for about 5 seconds, and relax. Do this 2-3 times.
- Tense your stomach. Do this 2-3 times.
- Now take 2-3 deep breaths and relax.
- Straighten your legs as much is comfortable for you. Pull your toes back, tense your calves. Do this 2-3 times if you are comfortable doing it again.
- Tense your buttocks. Do this 2-3 times.
- Now take 2-3 deep breaths and relax.
- Sit and feel the warmth, calmness, peacefulness and tell yourself something about yourself.

You don't have to be compulsive about how you do this technique. You can make up your own sequence of which muscles to tense and relax. Whatever you do is going to work for you.

MINDFULNESS
MINDFULNESS IS LEARNING TO PAY ATTENTION TO WHAT YOU ARE DOING AT THE PRESENT TIME AND KEEPING YOUR MIND FROM WANDERING

Mindfulness can be defined as paying attention to where you are and what you are doing and not having many thoughts running through your mind. The reality is everything you have learned so far qualifies as mindfulness. Everything you have learned will decrease the concentration of the hormones that interfere with your focusing and thinking clearly.

How often do we multi-task, doing one thing while thinking of 3 other things? Yes, I know, this was much easier to do successfully when we were younger. The concept of mindfulness is to clear the mind of extraneous thoughts so that attention can be directed to what you need to be doing. That is what all the techniques you have learned will help you do.

Everything you have learned will help you to focus and think clearly. You know why. It is because you are decreasing the concentration of the stress hormones that interfere with focusing and thinking clearly.

Why do you want to do to focus and become more efficient? If your mind is not wandering you will get things done more quickly. If you do this you will actually create time for yourself as you waste less time. What you do with that extra time is up to you. You can just relax or read a book or go for a walk, or do a project, or volunteer somewhere to help other people. Think of your own things. Or, if you want, work more and be more productive.

HELPFUL THINGS FOR YOU TO THINK ABOUT:

- Slow down so you can complete your thought before going on to a new thought. Remember, keeping your norepinephrine concentration low will help you to focus and think clearly. Trying to do too much can cause stress.
- Do one activity at a time and get it done before going on to a new activity. Trying to do more than one thing at a time may increase the amount of time it takes to get them done.
- Be conscientious and carefully consider your capabilities so that you don't take on tasks that will cause you stress. Conscientious people do more things to protect their health and engage in fewer activities that are risky. They are careful in planning for the future.
- When you are tired make sure you rest before engaging in additional activities. You will be able to think more clearly when you do this. Taking an afternoon nap is nothing to be embarrassed about.
- Don't be afraid to let go of activities that you find too difficult to do. Find activities that fit within your capabilities so that you can

clearly focus on them. If you need to do a difficult activity try to be mindful and just focus on that single activity.

• Let go of uncomfortable events from the past so that they no longer activate the stress reactive areas of your brain. Stewing over them will not do you any good. Expressive writing is a wonderful way to help you let go of troublesome things from your past.

Prioritize what you need to do or think about:

Maybe you would benefit by doing the most complicated first to get it out of the way and get it done when you are most fresh. That may help you relax as the other things you have to do next are easier.

Maybe you would benefit by doing the easiest first so you have a feeling of accomplishment. Getting the easier things out of the way lets you focus on the most difficult with fewer other things to think about.

Some people have better mental function earlier in the day, mid-day, or later in the day. Try to do difficult tasks when you function the best.

Don't waste time when you are tired, overwhelmed, and can't focus. Set the thing you are having difficulty with aside and come back to it later.

Don't be afraid to relax. Unfortunately, many people believe that they are wasting time if they relax. Remember, if you do something to decrease the concentration of your stress hormones you will find it easier to focus and you will become more efficient.

There are many ways to maintain full awareness from moment to moment. One of the simplest and most effective ways is to **PAY ATTENTION TO YOUR BREATHING**. Remember, that when we increase the amount of oxygen in our blood we are able to focus and think more clearly.

SOMETIMES YOUR MIND PERCEIVES SOMETHING AS STRESS WITHOUT YOU

BEING AWARE THAT IT IS PERCEIVING
SOMETHING AS STRESS

This is interesting and something you may have experienced. Most times when our brain perceives something as causing stress we are aware of it. We can't focus, we may say or do something that is inappropriate, we feel ourselves getting angry, our stomach feels funny or we may feel our face getting warm.

However, sometimes our brain will consider something to be stress but will not make us mentally aware of it. I know that this may seem a little weird, but it happens. When this occurs, stress hormones are having an effect on our health.

Importantly, when our brain is responding to stress but we are not cognitively aware of it, our body often will react in a specific way that can tell us our brain is responding to stress.

If you learn to recognize how our body responds to stress, even if you are not aware that your brain is responding to stress, you can use one of the relaxation techniques that you have found to be effective to calm your brain and lower the concentration of stress hormones and reduce the negative effects of stress on health.

Therefore, it is important to learn to use the signals from your body to help you know that your brain is responding to stress.

If you wish, someone can read the following to you or you can practice on your own: Sit comfortably

- Take 3 deep breaths to feel relaxed and calm
- Take your time, close your eyes if someone is reading this to you
- Now, think about something that causes you stress.
- Once you have identified something that causes you stress just think about it
- As you are thinking about it start to pay attention to how you feel
- Do you feel tightness in your forehead, jaw, or chin?

- What about the back of your neck, your shoulders, somewhere else?
- Do you find yourself holding your breath or clenching your fist?
- Do you feel a knot in your stomach?
- Pay attention to how your body is responding
- What you are feeling is how your body lets you know that your mind is causing an elevation of the stress hormones

It is important that you are aware of your body's reaction to stress so that you can use the signals to let yourself know that you are experiencing stress even though your brain does not make you aware of it. Once you are comfortable with stress coping techniques and you detect your body telling you that you are experiencing a stressor, you will want to use one of the coping techniques you are learning. The most common technique that is used for this is to take 1-3 deep breaths. That is what I do.

REMEMBER THIS (I know I'm repeating myself. It is intentional): Some people like to play the piano and others the violin. Some like to play football and others squash. People differ in the behaviors that are comfortable and enjoyable for them. You will find that we offer a variety of behaviors for you to use to help you cope with stress. This provides you with the opportunity to pick those that are comfortable and enjoyable for you. You do not need to use them all; rather you need to find what works for you so that it is something that you will use.

NOW LET'S TALK ABOUT SOME ASPECTS OF LIFE THAT CAN INFLUENCE MENTAL AND PHYSICAL HEALTH

WORK
ISSUES RELATING TO WORKING IN AN ENVIRONMENT WHERE YOU ARE UNHAPPY AND FEEL THAT THERE IS A LOT OF STRESS CAN HAVE AN AFFECT ON YOUR HEALTH

The psychological conditions of where you work can influence your health. Being in a workplace where you are comfortable with your environment, enjoy the people you are with, and have a good relationship with the supervisors who influence what and how you do your job, can have a positive effect on your health. Of course the opposite is true when you are in a workplace situation where you are unhappy.

- Health is impaired by having lots of responsibilities on the job but few resources and little cooperation from your coworkers
- There is little evidence that people who are heavily involved in their jobs and work long hours are more prone to heart disease if they ENJOY what they are doing and feel that they are appreciated.
- Those with the most career success are more likely to stay healthy and have longer life spans. On average the most successful men live five years longer than the least successful
- Those men who are unsuccessful in their careers and who are also unconscientious (as a child) have a significant increase in earlier mortality risk. You are likely to die sooner than you would if you were conscientious and successful.
- The most damaging sort of workplace stress is that arising from conflicts with other people rather than from the challenges and demands of the work itself. Having a poor relationship with your overbearing boss can lead to health problems, and not getting along with your coworkers can be harmful to health.
- Continually productive men and women who enjoy their successes, live longer than less successful employees who fret over their lack of success.
- Those who are the most disappointed with their achievements die the youngest.
- Stress at work increases the risk of heart disease and it is associated with more chemicals of inflammation in the blood. A healthier longer life is associated with less inflammation.

MARRIAGE AND DIVORCE

Marriage and becoming divorced can influence short and long-term health, in a positive or negative way. The issues are obvious and complex. For example, possibly the success of a marriage has to do with luck, sustained satisfaction, having the ability to compromise, changes in interests so you may grow closer or apart over time, or success or lack of success in one's work life.

A spouse can serve as a buffer against stress. After a bad day at work, having a loving friend on hand to relax with can be very calming. But what if your spouse nags, complains, and picks at the marital scabs as soon as you walk in the door? Maybe I don't have to go any further. From what you already know, you know the benefits of a calm supportive friendly environment in comparison to a hostile competitive marital environment.

Some thoughts about marriage are:

General

- Having a companion that you enjoy being with buffers loneliness
- Being married with a compatible partner may encourage you to be more physically active and buffer depression
- Being married and unhappy with the relationship may increase concentration of stress hormones and increase risk of depression and physical disease

General Findings Regarding Men

- Men who are in stable married relationships live the longest.
- Unmarried but healthy men who live a long life usually are found to maintain close relationships with friends and colleagues. Remember that loneliness has a negative effect on health.
- Many men tend to rely on their wives for their social ties and their emotional health. When these are lost due to divorce or death, the consequences often are a decreased quality of health. One factor that may affect health is that the male does not have anyone telling them to see a physician when they are not feeling well. Men tend to delay seeing a physician when they actually should be seeking care.
- Remarried men are less likely to live as long as steadily married men. They live longer than divorced men, but not as long as the steadily married men.

General Findings Regarding Women

- Women can more easily establish social and emotional ties with others. Therefore, those who are not in a stable marital relationship tend to do better than men
- The husband's marital happiness matters for his later health. This is not true for women
- If you are a single woman with a number of friends and an interesting life, don't think you need to follow the suggestion to get married (or remarried) to improve your health.
- Being single can often be just as healthy for a woman as being in a marriage, particularly if she has been stably, consistently single and has other fulfilling social relationships such as close friendships, meaningful memberships in organizations, and family ties.

It is easier for individuals to make a change in behavior if they have a spouse, friend, family member, who does it with them. Doing a change in behavior with someone else makes it more likely that the change will be sustained by both individuals.

BEFORE PROCEEDING LOOK AT THESE QUOTES FROM PEOPLE WHOSE NAME YOU MAY KNOW. I HAVE ADDED THE MEANING I FIND IN THE QUOTE. WHAT DOES IT MEAN TO YOU?

Think about this quote by Doris Lessing and how it may relate to you:

The great secret that all old people share is that you really haven't changed in seventy or eighty years. Your body changes, but you don't change at all. And, that, of course, causes great confusion.

What it means to me: Once again, one of my favorite and meaningful quotes is from Satchel Paige, "How old would you be if you didn't know how old you are". Never forget this quote and don't be confused about what is important. What is important is how old you feel and if you are mentally and physically healthy you will feel younger than your chronologic age. Yes, there are arthritic aches, physical endurance concerns, feelings of being frail. But what is important is feeling happy, having meaning in your life, being a part of something.

Think about this quote by Richard Armour and how it may relate to you:

I hope I have a young outlook. Since I have an old everything else, this is my one chance of having a bit of youth as part of me.

What it means to me: Once again, one of my favorite and meaningful quotes is from Satchel Paige, "How old would you be if you didn't know how old you are". Never forget this quote and don't be confused about what is important.

Think about this quote by Albert Schwitzer and how it may relate to you:

The tragedy of life is not in the fact of death. The tragedy of life is in what dies inside a man while he lives—the death of genuine feeling, the death of inspired response; the death of awareness that makes it possible to feel the pain or the glory of other men in oneself…No man need fear death: He need fear only that he may die without having known his greatest power—the power of his free will to give his life for others.

What it means to me: The last few words are a powerful statement. My interpretation is that the meaning of life is enhanced when you are doing things that are beneficial to others. To make life meaningful do things that make the quality of life of others better. That is something we each can take pride in.

Think about this quote by Norman Vincent Peale and how it may relate to you:

Live your life and forget you age.

What it means to me: Again, one of my favorite and meaningful quotes is from Satchel Paige, "How old would you be if you didn't know how old you are". The quote applies to what Norman Vincent Peale said.

THINK POSITIVE-PLACEBOS ARE REAL

I haven't said much about the effect of a placebo on your health. For our purpose a placebo is something that you respond to that should not cause a response but you believe it will. And then, something actually happens. For example, being given a sugar pill but being told that it is a pill that can relieve pain will, sometimes, relieve pain. You expect that whatever you have been given or whatever treatment is used will cause a response, and indeed, you respond.

Sometimes, in studies, people are given a medication that they found effective and later on they were given a sugar pill but were told that it is the medication. When this occurs they may have the same response to the sugar pill that they actually had to the medication. This would be called a placebo effect and is an example of the power of the mind.

As we did earlier, just put a big smile on your face. How do you feel?

Optimism is important for responding to a placebo. As your optimism that the treatment will be effective increases, response to a positive placebo expectation increases. Therefore, know that everything you are learning on this journey, about decreasing the response of your brain to stress and improving the quality of your health, is real. Read the comments from participants in our programs that I have already provided and provide later.

What am I saying: "Trust Me". It works!!!!

There are many studies that show the powerful effect of placebos. People with mild depression may respond as well to a placebo pill as to antidepressant medication. People with osteoarthritis of the knee may receive similar benefit from actual or faked surgical treatment. How much empathy (kindness and sensitivity) a physician shows to a patient may influence the response of the patient to the physician's care. There is evidence that the reduction of pain provided by a placebo works through lowering the response of the brain areas that respond to pain. The placebo response is not just in your imagination, there are effects on the brain.

Of course, at all times the proper medical or surgical treatment is essential. My point is that expecting a treatment to be effective can influence how effective it will be.

Therefore, my message is to expect everything I have told you to be effective. Indeed, everything I have told you will increase your ability to cope with stress with positive effects on your mind and body. If you don't believe it, you are less likely to achieve an increased ability to cope with stress.

LET ME MOTIVATE YOU ONCE MORE

When you increase your ability to cope with stress and keep the concentration of your stress hormones low, the following occur:

- There is an increase of amount of gray matter in your brain which is associated with more brain cells and better cognitive function
- The risk of depression is decreased as the number of neurons in the hippocampus of the brain are maintained
- The length of your telomeres (the caps on the end of your chromosomes) are longer and associated with better health and longevity
- Your immune system works appropriately
    - o reducing your risk of developing infectious disease
    - o responding better to immunization, for example, to flu vaccine
    - o reducing the likelihood of exacerbation of autoimmune diseases such as ulcerative colitis, Crohn's disease, psoriasis, multiple sclerosis, rheumatoid arthritis
- Blood pressure is better controlled and may be lower
- There is less accumulation of cholesterol in the walls of the blood vessels of the heart and atherosclerotic heart disease may be reduced
- Control of glucose for individuals with diabetes is easier to manage
- Focusing and thinking clearly is easier

RESTATING MY GUIDELINES FOR A LONG AND HEALTHY LIFE

- Children should grow up in a socially stable society having role models that use healthy lifestyle behaviors. Young children do not know what healthy behaviors are. They learn from those they love. If the important adults in a child's life use healthy behaviors, it is more likely that the child will grow up using those behaviors.
- Be part of a social network where you have others to talk to about personal issues, and with whom you engage in pleasurable activities so that your life is meaningful and interesting with goals that can be accomplished.
- You're never too old and it's never too late to increase your social interactions, and the returns can be significant in terms of life's quality and quantity
- Loneliness and the absence of friends can be stressful and unhealthy, unless you are seeking solitude, and are content with that life style
- Don't be critical of others. Avoid angry argument. Don't always try to get things your own way.
- Satisfaction with your career and your marital status enhances wellbeing
- Thoughtfully plan for the future with a sense of control and accomplishment
- Be conscientious by striving to keep your life organized and productive. Plan and have achievable goals. Those who are high in conscientiousness are more likely to use healthy lifestyle behaviors and have a good quality of mental and physical health and greater healthy longevity.

EFFECT OF STRESS ON YOUNGER VS OLDER ADULTS

Hopefully, both younger and older adults will have gone on this journey and learned how to increase their ability to cope with stress using the behaviors and techniques that have been provided. A logical question that may be asked is whether chronic stress is more likely to alter the health of younger or older adults.

As a general rule, older adults will be more susceptible to the health altering effects of stress. This may be due to their already having health alterations that have accumulated over many years and it will be easier for stress to alter tissue that is already altered. Other factors may be that younger people have more coping skills including more social interaction, are more physically active, or have immune systems that are functioning better.

Regardless, it is important for all, regardless of their age, to, at a minimum, be physically active, socially interactive, high in optimism and have a sense of humor.

Personally, I don't care if stress has more of an effect on young or older individuals. That's a question that maybe some researcher in a university would like to study so they can publish a paper. The reality is that it is important to start using the stress coping skills early in life and continue using them throughout life. Remember, children do not know what healthy or unhealthy behaviors are. They learn their behaviors from their role models, the parents and grandparents they love. That is why it is important for all of us to use healthy lifestyle behaviors so that we will have a meaningful effect on the quality of life of the children and grandchildren we care about.

However, regardless of how old you are, start increasing your ability to cope with stress NOW. It will be effective regardless of how old you are when you start doing this.

MY THOUGHTS ABOUT RETIREMENT

If you decide to retire the opportunity to make lifestyle changes that maintain or improve the quality of your health are often available. These may include sleeping later, a nap in the afternoon, long walks, learning things you wish you had learned earlier, volunteering in programs that help others, increasing your physical activity, spending more time with family, traveling to places you had often thought about visiting.

My belief is that maintaining and/or increasing social interaction is very helpful to your health when retired as it is likely that you will have the blues (depression) less. Not being lonely is extremely important. But remember, as I said earlier, if you are alone and not lonely, it is OK. However, you can be with people and still be lonely. When you are down in the dumps it is difficult to feel motivated to do something positive for yourself.

Going to a gym, finding a group to walk with (sometimes at an indoor shopping mall), engaging in volunteer activities (for example, volunteering at your local hospital), attending free lectures at a local university, attending classes at a local university that offers, for example, a Life Long Learning Program, visiting people who are ill at home through programs offered by places of worship, mentoring students through programs at schools, are examples of meaningful activities that one can engage in when they retire and have the available time. The bottom line is that I hope you don't just want to sit around and do nothing. Doing something that you enjoy and is providing benefit to others will have a meaningful positive effect on your mental and physical health. Remember, our goal is to stay healthy as we go thru the aging process and then to have a rapid demise.

A question that we often asked older participants in our group programs was, "What makes life meaningful for you"? The answer wasn't immediate. But eventually the answer was always the same, "Doing things for other people". Think about this if you consider retirement.

REPEATED ADVICE

- Please use relaxation techniques when you are calm. If you learn to do relaxation techniques when you are calm, the relaxation effect will be more likely to occur.

- The relaxation techniques need to be done regularly. Then, when you are under stress you will know what to do and it is more likely to be effective.
- Do you know when you are starting to get angry? Do you start to feel different when you start to get angry? Learn to do deep breathing when you start to get angry.

If you are comfortable, please share what you have learned in this journey of education and stress buffers with family, friends, colleagues. Helping others adds meaning to each of our life's.

PLEASE REMEMBER

- Increasing our ability to cope with stress by using behaviors and techniques that minimize the reactivity of the brain to stress can have a positive effect on your health and longevity.
- Learning to relax will not make you a less effective person or negatively affect your work performance. In fact, learning to relax will contribute to your being more efficient in your everyday life.
- We cannot make the stress in your life go away but by taking the journey that has been provided to you your brain will be less responsive to stress.
- By using your training from this journey, you and members of your family can lessen the influence of stress on your mental and physical health. You can do this by increasing your ability to cope with your stress.

MAKE YOUR LIFE MORE MEANINGFUL BY:

- Using what you learned all the time so that it becomes part of your life.
- Sharing this information with those who are important to you.

- Tell others how the quality of your life is better.
- Change your culture to one where healthy lifestyle behavior is used on a routine basis to enhance the quality of mental and physical health.
- Be patient
- Believe that you will succeed

Retake this journey as often as you wish. The goal is learning and using techniques and behaviors that can improve the quality of your health and quality of life. As your life changes for the better, those near and dear to you will reap the benefits as well

A GOOD THOUGHT: WHEN YOU ARE OLDER AND LOOK IN THE MIRROR, THE OLDER PERSON YOU MAY SEE THERE IS NOT YOU

PLEASE EMAIL ANY QUESTIONS TO: b.rabin100@gmail.com

TO FURTHER MOTIVATE YOU TO INCREASE YOUR ABILITY TO COPE WITH STRESS AND LET YOU KNOW THAT THIS JOURNEY REALLY WORKS THE FOLLOWING MESSAGES FROM PEOPLE WHO HAVE PARTICIPATED IN THIS STRESS COPING JOURNEY ARE PROVIDED

- I am immensely enjoying the benefits. It solidified my appreciation for the mind-body connection.
- After the training as I was walking towards my car I had the feeling that I had been at a day spa. I was very relaxed and had no pain in my back, which is not usually the case. I would like to incorporate these techniques in my daily life. Thank you.
- My heartfelt thanks for helping me learn to cope effectively with the stress I thought was so overwhelming. Life is so much better because of learning to cope with stress.
- The classes have taught me invaluable skills that will continue to enrich and enhance not only the quality of my existence, but also that of my family. I wish I had this opportunity earlier in life.

- I sleep better and can now reduce my reaction to stressful situations. This has also opened my eyes as to how detrimental stress is to our bodies, and our ability to maintain a greater quality of life as we age.
- One of my main realizations has been that I don't GIVE myself the time to relax! I'm always focused on some problem of the day. By realizing this, I have been providing myself the time to THINK about the things that are IMPORTANT to ME in my life. By giving myself this time to reflect, I have avoided making hasty decisions that would affect both my professional and personal lives. I feel that I have more of an overall sense of "well-being".
- I cannot express enough what a difference this class has made in my overall life.
- You introduced us to deep breathing and it has changed the way I got about my daily life. It has given me a tool to calm myself down in the most stressful situations (dealing with three young kids, sickness, etc). It's amazing that we all have the ability to do this and the results are so quick and profound.
- I forget to just breathe at times, and I didn't realize the impact this had on my health. I am now focusing on my breathing, which I needed with a busy schedule and the demands of a 10-month-old baby.
- I have taken the knowledge I received and have taught it to my husband who was very reluctant at first, but now I see him taking a few seconds to breathe before he deals with difficult situations, I even got him to Write
- Learning to breathe has helped me with stressful situations at home and at work.
- I am able to breathe when I get upset and not respond so quickly without thinking
- This past week I had a hospital procedure, as I lay on the operating table I was feeling anxious. Automatically I began to breathe and visualize. The procedure was done before I knew it and I realized how effective and useful the techniques I learned were.

- The class has taught me to use stress management techniques proactively instead of reactively. I still have stress in my life and in the workplace, but I am in control of my response to it.
- At home I've been sharing what I've learned with my family, neighbors and at church.
- I've noticed that I'm spending more time with friends and laughing more. I share what I learn with EVERYONE.
- The 15-minute writing method is a great way of screaming silently. I plan on using this method quite often.
- I know I feel better organized and better able to handle anything that is "thrown" at me at work and at home.
- One of my favorite things that I was taught was the writing lesson. It has always been a challenge for me to tell people how I felt, and I would usually write them a letter. But when I learned to write my anger out and then rip it out it made me feel so much better.
- Sometimes our jobs do create stress within our lives. Being able to recognize these stresses and manage them help us to be more productive in our jobs and our home life.
- By using guided imagery, I have begun to "permit" myself to take time to think about myself…and not work, family, etc…In doing so, I have begun to work on some of the issues that I have "uncovered".
- Before going to sleep I use the guided imagery.
- I am able to fall asleep easier and I don't wake up in the middle of the night as often. (And if I do wake up, I am able to fall asleep again.)
- Oh my goodness, I never could have imagined how effective that CD would be, besides relaxing, it totally took away my pain! I'm looking forward to listening again. Thank you so much.
- Everything I did the past couple of months were suggestions I got from your seminar. You helped me a lot. I now realize how important it is to manage your stress. Thank you for everything!
- I have fewer "down" times which don't last as long.
- My blood pressure which was regularly around 120/80 is now down to 100/74.

- At first I was hesitant about the "Wellness" Program that was offered to us, I knew I was stressed out, but I never thought anything could be done about it. Now I know it was truly a blessing and that the participants are truly thankful that this program has been offered to us, a wonderful "Gift".

- Just taking a few seconds to do something as easy as "breathing" can make such a difference in your day to ease the stressors. I also find myself enjoying the "moment" more often, taking the time to appreciate situations that are very important in my life.

- I practice the things I've learned regularly from belly breathing (my favorite, to smiling more, taking myself to a calm place and just moving around more (exercising).

- As soon as I feel stressed, I think oh I need to belly breathe and I do and instantly it helps to calm me.

- I have already experienced relief physically and emotionally from changes in my breathing alone.

- I went to my counselor yesterday; she said because of my stress techniques, it is NOT necessary to continue our sessions any longer. WOW! This should say it all.

- I sleep better and can now reduce my reaction to stressful situations. This has also opened my eyes as to how detrimental stress is to our bodies, and our ability to maintain a greater quality of life as we age.

- In my opinion, *everyone* should have the opportunity to experience this training.

- The classes have taught me invaluable skills that will continue to enrich and enhance not only the quality of my existence, but also that of my family. I wish this opportunity had come to me earlier in life.

- The littlest things would stress me out and I would say things that I really didn't want to say out loud and I use to be very impatient. I have learned to be way more laid back and to walk away and take a couple deep breaths

- Your class has helped me to cope with stresses of everyday life, and I will continue to use the strategies for wellness that you have shown me. I am richer for having had this experience.

- Benefits that I've experienced: much less aggressive driving; less bothered by rush hour traffic; able to be calmer in interactions with others; better listener; able through deep breathing to reduce post-surgical back pain; and improved sleep.
- In addition to the "advertised" benefits, I have had other positive side effects. I have had no cold sores (which I used to have almost constantly).
- I have greatly improved my relationships with my family and friends, and almost nothing which goes wrong seems to be a big deal to me anymore.
- I have noticed less of a need to eat sweet and salty snacks and an increased desire to walk and move around.
- I am teaching the techniques to my friend who has MS. She is falling asleep much easier and she has been able to handle her busy life with more energy and fewer flare-ups.
- At home, these techniques have helped me relate better with my children.
- I find myself continually using the deep breathing technique to get me through excessively busy times both at work and at home and deal with situations more calmly.
- At work I am not as reactionary, and I feel I am able to make better, more thoughtful decisions
- At home I am currently the primary care taker for my elderly parent who has Alzheimer's. I find that the class is helping me cope much better. I am able to let other family members know that I need help in a thoughtful more constructive way.
- I forget to just breathe at times, and I didn't realize the impact this had on my health. I am now focusing on my breathing, which I needed with a busy schedule and the demands of a 10-month-old baby.
- By using guided imagery, I have begun to "permit" myself to take time to think about myself...and not work, family, etc... In doing so, I have begun to work on some of the issues that I have "uncovered". · One of my main realizations has been that I don't GIVE myself the time to relax! I'm always focused on some problem of the day. By realizing this, I have been providing myself

the time to THINK about the things that are IMPORTANT to ME in my life. By giving myself this time to reflect, I have avoided making hasty decisions that would affect both my professional and personal lives. I feel that I have more of an overall sense of "well-being".

- I cannot express enough what a difference this class has made in my overall life.

- You introduced us to deep breathing and it has changed the way I got about my daily life. It has given me a tool to calm myself down in the most stressful situations (dealing with three young kids, sickness, etc). It's amazing that we all have the ability to do this and the results are so quick and profound.

- I have a 5-year-old son and I use the "blowing out the candles" technique with him. It does work, many times he forgets what he was upset about by the time he is done. He and I have deal that he will do this, but I must do it too when he sees me upset and he loves to remind me to "blow out the candles".

- Oh my goodness, I never could have imagined how effective that CD would be, besides relaxing, it totally took away my pain! I'm looking forward to listening again. Thank you so much.

- Everything I did the past couple of months were suggestions I got from your seminar. You helped me a lot. I now realize how important it is to manage your stress. Thank you for everything!

- I am immensely enjoying the benefits. It solidified my appreciation for the mind-body connection.

- After the training as I was walking towards my car I had the feeling that I had been at a day spa. I was very relaxed and had no pain in my back, which is not usually the case. I would like to incorporate these techniques in my daily life. Thank-you

Printed in the United States
By Bookmasters